Electronic Communication Aids

Selection and Use

This book is dedicated to my clients,
who have taught me most of what I know.

Electronic Communication Aids
Selection and Use

Iris Fishman, M.A.

Augmentative Communication Specialist

Cerebral Palsy Center of Fairfield County
Bridgeport, Connecticut

A College-Hill Publication
Little, Brown and Company
Boston/Toronto/San Diego

College-Hill Press
A Division of
Little, Brown and Company (Inc.)
34 Beacon Street
Boston, Massachusetts 02108

Library of Congress Cataloging in Publication Data
Main entry under title:

Fishman, Iris, 1951–
  Electronic communication aids and techniques.

  Includes index.
  1. Communication devices for the disabled.
2. Computerized self-help devices for the handicapped.
I. Title
HV1569.5.F57   1987   621.38   86-28337
ISBN 0-316-28397-5

Printed in the United States of America

Contents

Preface

This book is a practical guide to the selection and use of electronic communication aids. It is written primarily for those involved in the treatment or care of individuals who are unable to meet all their communication needs through speech or writing. Because the book contains basic information on augmentative communication techniques and aids as well as suggestions and recommendations for clinical applications, the book is appropriate for students of speech pathology, occupational and physical therapies, special education, and other related fields, as well as for practicing professionals. Families of speech/writing-impaired individuals, who play very important advocacy roles, will also benefit from this book, as, of course, will the consumer—the augmentative communication aid user. Also, this book can give administrators of programs and funding agencies for the physically disabled useful insights into the aids that they are so frequently asked to purchase.

Given the recent advances in technology, the task of learning about electronic aids often seems overwhelming, particularly in view of the limited information available about the capabilities of these aids, the appropriate means of selecting them, and the individuals who can benefit from them. Sometimes, a specific aid is selected based on what is familiar or readily available. When a selection is made on this basis, the aid frequently becomes an unused reminder of a costly error and a disappointed client.

Because technology is rapidly changing, this book provides a foundation of knowledge upon which currently available and future aids can be evaluated. The book provides guidelines and examples designed to help the professional to determine whether an individual needs an electronic aid and the type of aid needed, to compare aids and avoid common mistakes regarding their selection, and to implement strategies for their effective use.

This book is divided into seven parts. In Chapters 1 and 2 (of Part I), electronic communication aids are defined in terms of their relationship to all augmentative means of communication. The individuals who use these aids are described, and the roles of the various professionals who are involved in selecting, manufacturing and selling aids, and implementing their use are described. In Chapter 3, the realities of electronic aids are discussed.

In Chapters 4 and 5, the communication needs of speech/writing-impaired individuals are described, along with dimensions of augmentative components that must be evaluated in determining these needs. An example of a communication needs assessment provides an illustration of how communication needs are determined.

The third part (Chapters 6 through 9) describes the output of communication aids, including attention-getting, visual selection, speech output, visual display or print, as well as their capabilities and limitations and methods of determining which output can best meet a particular communication need. Examples of how these outputs are used by speech/writing-impaired individuals are also included.

Parts IV, V, and VI describe the selection techniques, vocabulary capabilities, and portability features of augmentative communication aids. Guidelines, examples, comparisons between nonelectronic and electronic aid features, and evaluations of each of these features will assist the reader in selecting the best aid for a particular individual.

Part VII addresses the roles that microcomputers and dedicated aids play in providing communication needs. Chapter 18 presents the difference between computer-based and dedicated communication aids, along with guidelines and examples to assist in deciding between them. The need for providing the speech/writing-impaired individual with effective means of communication as well as with access to computers to pursue educational and vocational goals is stressed. To conclude, examples of the impact of rapidly changing technology on the decision-making process are presented and discussed.

Electronic Communication Aids: Selection and Use was written by a professional directly involved with the day-to-day issues concerning selection and implementation of augmentative communication aids for severely speech/writing-impaired children and adults. The examples, case histories, suggested guidelines, and procedures are based on daily experiences with this population and these aids. Thus, this book is designed to provide a practical approach to understanding, selecting, and using electronic communication aids so that speech/writing-impaired individuals can receive maximum benefit from them.

Acknowledgments

This book could not have been written without the help and support of several people, whom I would like to thank. Without the guidance and encouragement of Janice LaRouche, I might have never begun. Without the patient support of my husband, Jay, I might never have finished. Throughout, Berenice Hoffman assertively represented me.

I would also like to thank Dr. Florence Edelman and Dr. Gregg Vanderheiden for their review of the manuscript. Dr. Vanderheiden, whose work has greatly influenced my professional life, devoted an enormous amount of time to the review and editing of this book, and his contributions are reflected throughout.

My experiences working at the Cerebral Palsy Center of Fairfield County in Bridgeport, Connecticut, and at Goldwater Memorial Hospital, New York University Medical Center, in New York City, have provided the basis for a great deal of the material in this book. I owe a tremendous thanks to the staff and clients at these facilities, and to Barry Buxbaum, Executive Director at the Cerebral Palsy Center, who allowed me to take the time I needed to complete this project.

Finally, I would like to thank the professionals and the companies in the field of augmentative communication who endured my persistent phone calls and letters and who generously provided me with so much of the material that is essential to this book.

"It is as though the darkness had
Speech of silver words...."

Orrick Johns

PART I

Defining Terms, Roles, and Realities

1

What Are Electronic Communication Aids?

COMPONENTS OF AN OVERALL AUGMENTATIVE COMMUNICATION SYSTEM

Electronic communication aids are one of many specialized augmentative components used by severely speech/writing-impaired individuals comprising an overall augmentative communication system. Augmentative components, however, are also used by able-bodied persons. Facial expression, gestures, changes in body position, laughter, crying and writing are standard techniques and aids (components) that play as important a part in conveying meaning as speech. In many situations, they become even more important, as in a very noisy environment, such as a subway or disco; in a quiet environment, such as a library or theatre; or in a country where an individual does not speak the language.[1]

Individuals who are unable to meet all their communication needs through speech and/or writing rely more heavily on standard techniques and use them more frequently than do able-bodied persons. The greater the speech/writing impairment, the more these techniques will be used to supplement residual speech/writing abilities.

In addition, a number of specialized augmentative components have been developed to extend and enhance the use of standard techniques. For those who use gesture, more systematic gesture systems have been developed. Another reason for the development of specialized components is that individuals with severe impairments often cannot effectively use standard techniques; for example, those with limited use of their hands cannot use gestures.[1] Thus, a speech/writing impaired individual's overall augmentative communication system consists of standard techniques and aids also used by able-bodied individuals, and specialized components developed for persons whose needs cannot be met through standard components alone. These specialized components include symbols, techniques, aids, strategies, and skills.

Symbols

Symbols, representing the thoughts and ideas the individual wants to express, may be classified as aided or unaided. Unaided symbols are those that the individual produces[2]; for example, American Sign Language, fingerspelling, and spoken language.

For those individuals who do not have the physical ability to produce symbols, aided symbols may be used. These can be objects or graphic representations, for instance, pictures, photos, or the alphabet, which the individual can select from some type of aid, such as a display or chart. Graphic symbols are used with communication aids because they can be stored or displayed. They can also be used to produce a permanent copy of an individual's communication and can be written or printed on electronic displays or paper.[2]

Transmission Techniques

An individual can physically transmit a message through either production-based or selection-based techniques. With production-based techniques, the individual actually *produces* the symbols used for communication; e.g., the oral-respiratory system is used to produce and transmit speech, or the person produces yes/no responses, facial expressions, body gestures, signs, etc. An artificial larynx or a microphone and writing with a pen are examples of aided production-based techniques.

The advantage of production-based techniques is the user's extremely large vocabulary, because any item that can be remembered is accessible to the user. For example, the only limitation to using sign language is the individual's vocabulary. In order to use a production-based technique, the user must have good physical control, e.g., good upper extremity ability and control of facial expression to use American Sign Language.[2]

Selection-based techniques require much less physical control because, to form a particular message, the user selects the desired symbols from a predetermined set, using one of various selection techniques; e.g., direct selection, where the user points to a symbol. In contrast with production-based techniques, the individual's access to language with a selection-based technique is limited to those items in the selection set. The exception to this is when the alphabet or its equivalent is used, which allows the individual to spell anything he or she wants to express. This would be considered a production-selection based technique.[2]

Selection-based techniques may or may not involve the use of an aid. For example, when a partner scans items on a communication board until the desired item is reached and the impaired individual stops the partner, this is an *aided* scanning technique. If the partner names a series of items (Do you want this? This? This?) until the individual indicates the desired one, this is an *unaided* scanning technique.

Aids

An aid is a physical object or device that assists communication. As discussed above, symbols and techniques can be implemented through aids. A communication aid is a physical object or device that displays or stores a set of graphic symbols which the individual selects through one of several selection techniques. It can be classified as nonelectronic or electronic. Nonelectronic aids have no electronic or mechanical parts and typically consists of some type of symbol selection display. In addition to this display, an electronic aid has one or more electronic components requiring an outlet or batteries for power. This component allows the aid to store items or produce output.

Strategies and Skills

A strategy is a specific way of using aids or techniques more effectively for specific purposes. There are many strategies that can increase the speed and effectiveness of communication once the user knows them.[2] For example, if an individual uses an electronic aid that displays the letters of the alphabet as he or she selects them, speed of communication can be increased by the person spelling the *abbreviations* of certain words rather than the entire word.

A skill is an ability that is developed over time with frequent use. In order to use strategies effectively, an individual must practice the skills involved.[1] For example, to effectively use an abbreviation strategy, the individual must practice discriminating between those partners who will understand the abbreviations and those who will not, selecting which words to abbreviate, spelling the abbreviations, etc.

Strategies and the skills needed to use them are as important a component as are the transmission technique, the aid, and the symbols. The most successful users of augmentative communication systems are those who have either been taught effective strategies or have discovered them themselves.[1]

FEATURES OF COMMUNICATION AIDS

The features of communication aids include output, selection technique, vocabulary capability, and portability.

Output

This refers to the mode of presentation of the messages or vocabulary items represented by the symbols selected by the individual. There are five modes of output.

1. Attention-getters.
     This can be any type of noise, alarm, or auditory signal.
2. Visual selection.
     This can be nonelectronic or electronic. In a nonelectronic mode, the individual communicates a message to the partner through indicating a selected item on an aid's display through one of several selection techniques. An electronic visual selection aid directly displays a selected item to the partner through some type of indicator; e.g., a flashing light or arrow.[3]

3. Speech output.

A selected message is spoken through a synthesizer or other device.

4. Visual display.

Symbols, usually letters of the alphabet, are displayed across a screen as the individual selects them and disappear when the aid's power is shut off.

5. Printed display.

Symbols, usually letters of the alphabet, are permanently printed on paper as the individual selects them.

Selection Technique

This refers to the techniques used to select desired items, that is, direct selection, scanning, and directed scanning. In addition, encoding can be used with either direct selection or scanning.

Vocabulary Capability

This refers to the capability of the aid to allow the individual to have the vocabulary items that he wants displayed on or stored in the aid.

Portability

This refers to the size, shape, weight and source of power of the aid, all of which determine the ability of the aid to be transported by a particular individual.

SOME DIFFERENCES BETWEEN THE FEATURES OF NONELECTRONIC AND ELECTRONIC AIDS

One major difference between nonelectronic and electronic aids is the degree to which their features can be customized for a particular individual. The nonelectronic aid is usually custom-designed for a particular speech-impaired individual in terms of selection technique, symbol set, and portability by the speech pathologist working with him or her in conjunction with other professionals such as the occupational and physical therapists, the teacher, etc. In many cases, a family member or friend designs and constructs the aid. As much as possible, the speech-impaired individual is also included in the design process. Although an electronic aid can be custom-made for a particular individual, it is usually manufactured for a general group of individuals and its use may be limited to those individuals with particular abilities, e.g., those who can directly select items, those who can spell.

Another difference between nonelectronic and electronic aids is their ability to meet communication needs other than conversation. Nonelectronic aids can only be used for face-to-face conversation, i.e.,conversation where a partner is present and in close physical proximity to the aid user. In addition to face-to-face conversation, many electronic aids can be used for conversation at a distance from the partner, for preparing messages, for writing, and for providing access to computers and other electronic devices.

CATEGORIES OF ELECTRONIC AIDS

Electronic aids can be classified into three categories: dedicated aids, microcomputers, and adapted aids. Dedicated aids have been designed and manufactured specifically to be used as communication aids for severely speech/writing-impaired individuals. Microcomputers, designed to perform a number of functions for able-bodied individuals, can also be used as communication aids in conjunction with a custom-designed software/hardware package. Other dedicated devices, designed and manufactured to perform a specific function for able-bodied people (e.g., a language translator, an educational toy for children, or a calculator) can also be used by some speech/writing impaired individuals as communication aids.

For the purposes of this book, the general term *electronic communication aid* will be used to include all three types of aids unless otherwise indicated. Currently, over 50 such aids are commercially available; i.e., systems currently available and distributed in the United States.[4] There are also countless aids in varying stages of research and development.

REFERENCES

1. Vanderheiden, G. and Yoder, D.E. (in press). In S.W. Blackstone (Ed.), *Augmentative Communication: An Introduction.* Rockville, MD: American Speech and Hearing Association.
2. Vanderheiden, G. and Lloyd, L. (in press), in S.W. Blackstone (Ed.), *Augmentative Communication: An Introduction*, Rockville, MD: American Speech and Hearing Association.
3. Kraat, A. W. (1982). Output modes available in communication devices. Presented at Communication Aids Workshop, West Lake Ohio.
4. Kraat, A. W. and Sitver-Kogut, M. (1985). Features of commercially available communication aids. Prentke Romich Co., Phonic Ear, Don Johnston Developmental Equipment, Words Plus, Inc.

2   Who Is Involved?

SPEECH/WRITING-IMPAIRED INDIVIDUALS

Speech-impaired individuals are unable to meet all their communication needs through speech because of an accident, illness, or other condition. The terms *nonvocal, nonoral, nonverbal,* or *nonspeaking*, often used to describe these individuals, generally are misleading because they imply that the individual is totally unable to speak. In fact, a very large number of individuals who use augmentative means of communication have partial functional speech.

Speech-impaired individuals can exhibit a wide range of speech abilities. For example, one individual may have severe respiratory and articulatory impairments resulting in speech that is unintelligible to unfamiliar persons but understood by very familiar persons. Another may have adequate articulatory control but be unable to produce voice; some familiar persons may be able to "lipread." A third individual may be totally unable to speak.

A speech-impaired individual may also have an impairment of the upper extremities, which prevents him or her from using gestural systems or limits the use of these systems. For example, an individual may have adequate ability to use sign language with familiar partners who recognize his particular style of signs, may be unable to produce signs intelligible enough for a stranger to understand, even if the stranger is familiar with the sign system the individual is using.

The ability to write may also be affected by upper extremity impairment. Because of the emphasis placed on augmenting speech, the need to write is often forgotten. However, taking notes, doing assignments, composing letters, performing calculations, and performing many other tasks is as important a communication need for many individuals as speaking. Many individuals use writing to such a great extent to organize thoughts and develop ideas that they cannot effectively think without it. For those who want to pursue academic goals, writing is essential.[1]

The need to write is often forgotten with speech/writing-impaired children, who are sent to school with elaborate communication boards or with electronic aids producing speech output but without any means of writing. These children are being asked to learn by just listening and remembering; no wonder that many of them never learn how to spell or read.[1]

In addition to individuals who are both speech and writing impaired are those with adequate speech but whose writing abilities are impaired. Both groups of individuals will need to use special augmentative techniques and aids to supplement their writing abilities.

Many different conditions, illnesses, syndromes and traumas can result in a speech/writing impairment. This diversity of etiology results in a wide range of ages among speech/writing-impaired individuals as well as a wide range in age of onset of the impairment and prognosis for recovery or improvement of abilities. An individual either can be born with a congenital disorder that affects the development of speaking and/or writing or can acquire the impairment at any point in life. The speech/writing impairment can last for the individual's entire life or only for a period of time. The condition may improve or worsen. All of these factors will determine the intervention program for a particular individual. For example, intervention with a 3-year-old cerebral palsied child who has never developed functional speech will be different from intervention with a 65-year-old man with a degenerative disease that has affected his speech abilities for the past year.

Primary disorders that may result in the need for special techniques and aids to augment speech and/or writing abilities[3] include congenital conditions, acquired disabilities, progressive diseases, viral diseases, and temporary conditions.[2]

Thus, speech/writing-impaired persons exhibit a wide range of speech, physical, cognitive, sensory, and perceptual abilities. A determination of the augmentative techniques and aids to be used with an individual must be based on his or her particular communication abilities and needs.

COMMUNICATION PARTNERS

A communication partner is a person with whom the speech/writing-impaired individual communicates. The term *partner* implies a mutual sharing of communication, where either participant can send or receive a message. To clarify the difference between the individual transmitting a message through an augmentative technique and the person receiving the message, the terms *message sender* and *receiver* are sometimes used.

Partners can be categorized by their personal familiarity or interpersonal relationship with the individual. Some partners are very familiar and others less so, depending on their frequency of interaction and length of time they have known the individual. A stranger is a person who is personally unfamiliar with the individual.

Partners can also be categorized by whether they have been trained to understand and use any of the individual's augmentative aids or techniques. A trained partner is one who understands a particular communication symbol set, technique, or aid the individual uses. The degree to which prior training is important depends upon the obviousness of the technique or symbol set being used as well as the intelligibility of the output.

For example, if an individual is using an electronic aid producing speech output, no prior training is needed to understand it. If the individual is using a nonelectronic aid that involves pointing to a number code corresponding to pictures, the technique is less obvious and more training will be required of the partner.[3]

Some partners may be trained to use certain techniques but not others with an individual. For example, a mother is trained in communicating with her speech-impaired child through yes/no questions, facial expression, and eye pointing but is untrained with the eye gaze system set up for the child in school.

A *familiar untrained partner* can be personally familiar with an individual but not be trained to use any augmentative techniques or aids. Perhaps the partner is unable or unwilling to spend the time in training or no one is available to train the partner. For example, a physician who is very familiar with a speech-impaired patient may only communicate with that patient through an interpreter because the physician never was trained to use the patient's nonelectronic encoding system. However, most people who are familiar with a speech-impaired individual and come into regular contact with him or her will usually have been trained to use some communication technique, even if it is limited to yes/no questioning.

WHOSE FIELD IS THIS ANYWAY?

According to the American Speech and Hearing Association (ASHA)[4], speech pathologists should be primarily responsible for augmentative means of communication, and the association has established guidelines for the role of its members in this field. In reality, however, the profession that takes responsibility for augmentative communication varies in each facility. In some places, the responsibility falls to speech pathology, while in others, it falls to occupational therapy, special education, social work, or any profession that has recognized the need for these services.

The reason for this variation is because so little training is offered to professionals in this area that, in many cases, no one is particularly expert. In addition, the field of augmentative communication involves the participation of many disciplines, all of which are interdependent. No one discipline can work in isolation to provide a successful communication system for a speech-impaired individual.

The primary professionals involved in this field include speech pathologists and occupational and physical therapists. Depending on where the service is being provided, a rehabilitation engineer may be involved along with a special education teacher, a social worker, a psychologist, a nurse, and a physician. A vendor or manufacturer of electronic aids will also be involved at some point. In addition, the severely speech-impaired individual, his or her family, and other communication partners must be included.

There often is confusion about the roles that each profession plays in providing a communication system. Of all the roles, that of the speech pathologist is clearest. A speech pathologist is responsible for determining candidacy of a speech/writing-impaired individual for a communication aid; determining his or her communication needs; assessing language, cognitive, and visual abilities; selecting an aid; training the individual and communication partners in its use; etc. He or she is usually the coordinator of the team that provides the overall communication system.

In a school, the special education teacher can also play a major role in coordinating the speech-impaired individual's communication program. Since the teacher interacts with the individual for most of the day and is the one who needs to communicate with him or her most frequently, the speech pathologist and teacher need to work together closely. Very often, the teacher designs a nonelectronic aid, adds vocabulary items, trains the individual, and does many of the language-related tasks traditionally thought of as the speech pathologist's role.

The roles of physical and occupational therapy overlap or are interchangeable, depending on the policy of each facility. In general, occupational/physical therapy is responsible for positioning the speech-impaired individual to optimize his or her physical abilities, determining the best selection technique to be used with a communication aid, and positioning the communication aid and/or control switch.

In some places, physical therapy is responsible for positioning, while occupational therapy deals with upper extremity functioning. In other places, occupational therapy positions individuals in wheelchairs, while physical therapy positions them in bed. In most places, there may be only a physical or an occupational therapist to do everything. Regardless of who performs which function, if the occupational/physical therapy functions are not performed, the speech pathology functions are curtailed, since physical control is crucial to the use of a communication aid.

Social work and psychology also play important roles in implementing the use of communication aids. Very often, a social worker investigates funding sources and writes and submits requests for funding of specific aids. In rehabilitation settings, a discharge planning department also may be involved. Additionally, psychologists willing to counsel severely speech-impaired individuals can greatly influence whether a communication aid is used successfully.

Along with the social worker, the nurse or doctor is often the first professional person to see the speech-impaired person. When these professionals know where to refer such an individual for assistance, it can mean the difference between receiving appropriate services or not.

Often there is confusion concerning when it is appropriate to work with the vendor of electronic aids and when to work with the manufacturer. The manufacturer designs and produces the electronic aid and often is the only one who can repair or make modifications to it. The manufacturer also can provide detailed information on the capabilities and operation of the aid. The manufacturer usually employs rehabilitation engineers who design electronic aids and control interfaces. In addition, manufacturers often can adapt their commercially available items if they cannot be used by an individual as is.

The vendor represents the manufacturer to the consumer. A vendor may represent one manufacturer or several and have a large inventory of aids or only a few. The vendor usually is based locally and also sells other medical equipment: wheelchairs, leg braces, etc. It is very rare to find a vendor who specializes only in electronic communication aids.

The vendor will usually bring the aid in question to a facility, demonstrate it free of charge, and answer basic questions about its operation. Vendors vary greatly in their knowledge, and it may be necessary to call the manufacturer for certain information about a particular aid.

Because of the lack of training in this area, at times professionals overlap in their functions. Also, at times, one professional knows more about another's work than the other professional does. For example, a speech pathologist who worked in a facility that focused on augmentative communication and later moved to a facility that focused on other methods, will know something about the roles of all professionals involved in augmentative communication, not just the role of speech pathology. Having worked with occupational therapists who provide communication aids, the speech pathologist may know more about positioning and assessing physical abilities than do the therapists at the new facility. In such a case, the speech pathologist must assume a teaching role without alienating his or her new colleagues.

Thus, the professional who sees the need to provide augmentative communication services should initiate them. Augmentative communication is not the sole responsibility of one profession. Rather, it belongs to all health professionals.

REFERENCES

1. Vanderheiden, G. (1983). Non-conversational communication technology needs of individuals with handicaps. *Rehabilitation World*, Vol. 7, p.8.
2. Vanderheiden, G. and Yoder, D.E. (in press). In S.W. Blackstone (Ed.), *Augmentative Communication: An Introduction*. Rockville, MD: American Speech and Hearing Association.
3. Vanderheiden, G. and Lloyd, L. (in press). In S.W. Blackstone (Ed.), *Augmentative Communication: An Introduction*. Rockville, MD: American Speech and Hearing Association.
4. ASHA Ad Hoc Committee on Communication Processes and Nonspeaking Persons. (1980). Non-speech communication: A position paper. *ASHA*, Vol. 2, No. 4, p. 268.

3

The Realities of Electronic
Communication Aids

**THE EFFECT OF
ELECTRONIC AIDS ON
SPEECH ABILITY**

Many speech/writing-impaired individuals, their families, and the professionals who work with them resist using electronic aids, although the individuals could benefit from them. This resistance results from the belief that an electronic communication aid, or an augmentative technique or aid of any kind, will prevent the severely speech-impaired individual from developing or regaining speech abilities. When the individual has a degenerative condition, it is often feared that the technique will hasten degeneration.

In fact, when properly implemented, the use of any augmentative technique or aid is part of the individual's overall communication system, which includes using whatever speech abilities he or she has, whatever standard techniques (gesture, facial expression, and pointing) can be used, and special augmentative components. The individual who has the potential for developing speech also should continue to receive such treatment.[1]

Several studies have demonstrated that using augmentative techniques and aids increases the intelligibility of speech where there is that potential. By providing another approach to communication, the pressure is removed from the severely speech-impaired individual, who relaxes and is better able to communicate through whatever speech abilities he or she has. As a result, the individual's speech is more fluent and intelligible. Another reason is that when using an augmentative means of communication, the speech-impaired individual can cue his or her communication partner as to the general topic, which results in making partially intelligible speech more intelligible.[1]

Clinical experience has demonstrated that using augmentative techniques and aids provides greater motivation to work toward developing speech. For many individuals, it is the first time they have been able to successfully communicate and to control their environment. This success motivates them to develop and use any speech abilities they may have. An augmentative technique also may motivate the individual who has an acquired condition to try to regain speech abilities. And, it may motivate the individual with a degenerative condition to retain those abilities for as long as possible.

In general, a severely speech-impaired individual who has a desire to communicate would not choose to use an augmentative means of communication over speech; it is far too slow and inefficient. Rather than becoming dependent on the technique, a common occurrence is for the individual to first attempt to use whatever speech abilities are available and then to persist in using speech, even when it is not understood after several attempts.

Thus, resistance to electronic aids, and to all augmentative communication techniques and aids, is based on the belief that their use mandates an either/or situation: the individual *either* uses speech *or* uses an augmentative technique or aid. To the contrary, the severely speech-impaired individual's overall communication system consists of multiple techniques and aids, which, where possible, includes speech.

AVOIDING DISAPPOINTMENT WITH ELECTRONIC AIDS

While resistance to using electronic aids has prevented some individuals from using them, unrealistic expectations about the capabilities of these aids invariably leads to disappointment with them. The most common expectation is that the electronic aid will transform the speech-impaired individual into a speaking person.

In reality, just as an individual who is a paraplegic and given a wheelchair cannot be equal in physical ability to a person who is able to walk, a speech-impaired individual with a communication aid cannot be equal in speech ability to a person who is able to speak. While electronic aids provide independence in communication, they are not as rapid or as efficient as speech. In many cases, the individual's nonelectronic aid or unaided communication techniques are far more efficient.

Another expectation is that once an electronic aid is selected, the speech-impaired individual will use it for the rest of his or her life. In reality, as technology changes and the individual's needs or abilities change, different aids will be required. In addition, as discussed in the previous section, the individual's overall communication system will consist of a number of techniques and aids because no single aid or technique can provide for all communication needs.

Finally, many professionals believe that their responsibility is to select an electronic aid, obtain funding for it, and train the individual to become proficient in producing messages with the aid. They think that once this is accomplished, the necessity for their involvement is over.

In fact, in addition to providing an aid and the training to produce messages, an individual also must be given strategies to increase speed and effectiveness in communication. Continuing involvement also is essential for things as minor as assistance in trouble shooting or as major as reassessment for a new aid. In order to be successfully used, the professionals working with these individuals must devote time to develop communication strategies, to train the individuals to use them, to maintain the aids, and to continually assess the individual's communication needs. Speech-impaired individuals are never totally discharged from treatment because, to some degree, they always will need the services of an augmentative communication specialist.

Thus, when applying for funding for an aid, the acquisition cost is not the only cost to be requested. It is also important to include funds for training, aid maintenance, and modification. If funding for services and training is not secured, it is unlikely that the individual will have an aid that can be used effectively.

For these reasons, beginning the evaluation for an electronic aid, an awareness of these factors is necessary to develop realistic expectations about their capabilities. While the use of an electronic aid will not transform the speech-impaired individual into a speaking person, when selected and implemented properly, it can provide an independent, functional means of communication for certain needs.

THE COST OF ELECTRONIC AIDS

A common complaint made about electronic aids, usually by funding agencies, is that they are too expensive. While they do cost more than nonelectronic aids, the total cost of an aid or technique must be considered rather than only its purchase cost. Continuing costs for maintenance, training, and assistance required to use the technique or aid must also be included. Nonelectronic aids have low purchase costs but very high costs for an individual who needs to do any independent work or writing[1]. The cost of an assistant to act as scribe and interpreter is far greater than the cost of any electronic aid.

In many cases, the lack of an electronic aid defeats the purpose of the funds spent on an individual's rehabilitation or education process. Thousands of dollars a year are spent on educating severely disabled children, and yet they may not be given effective means for participating in that education. Insurance may pay for many hours of therapy and rehabilitation attendants but may not fund an aid that ultimately decreases costs by making the individual less dependent on others.

The long-term effects on the individual of not having an electronic aid also must be considered. When an individual is forced to depend on others to make phone calls, write letters, etc., and is severely limited in communicating with others, this can result in mental and emotional problems. Also, if such individuals are placed in life-threatening situations, they may be unable to inform unfamiliar caretakers of swallowing difficulties, feeding techniques, symptoms or locations of pain, etc.

Thus, the cost of an electronic aid must be compared with the cost of caring for an individual who may become emotionally and physically debilitated as a result of dependency and isolation. The intial high cost of an electronic aid may prevent additional, more expensive health care costs. In many cases, an electronic aid allows an individual to rejoin the community or earn an income, lessening health costs even further.[2]

THE NEED FOR BOTH NONELECTRONIC AND ELECTRONIC AIDS

As a result of the technological revolution in augmentative communication, professionals often view electronic aids as necessary and nonelectronic aids as unnecessary, or they may make the mistake of choosing between these aids. In fact, selecting these aids is never really an either/or decision. An individual with an electronic aid will always need a nonelectronic aid, not just as backup but for those situations in which the nonelectronic aid is more effective. Nonelectronic aids should be introduced *in addition to* electronic aids not instead of them. Each aid is on a continuum with the others, and they are complementary to each other.

This is similar to the use of motorized and manual wheelchairs. On the one hand, a motorized wheelchair will be better in certain environments because it will allow a particular individual to travel independently; e.g., from class to class in school. On the other hand, there will be occasions when that person cannot use the motorized chair; for instance, the chair may need repairs, or it may not be easily maneuvered over the carpeting through hallways.

Thus, one chair is not better than another at all times. The motorized chair is better in particular environments, while in others the manual chair is better. Rather than choosing between two chairs, the individual needs both, each to be used in different situations.

In a similar manner, electronic aids are not better than nonelectronic aids. In certain situations, a nonelectronic aid may be more effective, while in other situations an electronic aid will be preferable. For each individual, a decision must be made as to when each type of aid as well as other augmentative means of communication are indicated. This is essential in order to provide an effective overall communication system.

EXAMPLE USING NONELECTRONIC AND ELECTRONIC AIDS

Jane, Olive, and Mary were quadriplegic and severely speech impaired due to disorders they acquired later in life. Jane, 48 years old, and Olive, 60 years old, both had had brainstem CVAs; while Mary, 21 years old, had had viral encephalitis. They all lived in a large, chronic care rehabilitation facility.

Each woman had a nonelectronic communication aid. Jane used an alphabet board whose letters were scanned by her communication partner in a row-column fashion. Olive used a light beam, mounted to her forehead, to indicate letters on an alphabet board. Mary used eye gaze to indicate a code on a display, placed on her laptray, that stood for the letters of the alphabet.

Some staff in the facility knew how to communicate with Jane, Olive, and Mary, using their nonelectronic aids. The staff included a speech pathologist and communication assistant, who had designed and implemented the aids, and a psychologist, a social worker, an occupational therapist, and the head nurse of the ward on which they lived. The nonelectronic aids provided a rapid means of conversation with these partners.

However, this meant that only six people in the entire facility knew how to communicate with these women. Staff members who were not specifically assigned to them, and so did not learn to use the nonelectronic aids, could not communicate with them except by means of yes/no questions, guesses, or through one of those who knew how to communicate. Outsiders, such as family, friends, and volunteers, did not visit frequently and were not able to use the aids effectively. Other patients in the hospital who could not indicate the items on the alphabet board, see the display, or who were unable to read also could not communicate with these women.

One of the most frustrating aspects of using the nonelectronic aids was communication in a psychotherapy group to which the three women belonged. There were a total of ten members in this group, all of whom were speech impaired and used nonelectronic aids. Each member had a buzzer to signal the desire to speak, but then was dependent on a staff member to interpret the message to the rest of the group. The group members sat in a circle and staff members sat between the group members in case someone wanted to speak.

Although volunteers and students were always coaxed to help, there never seemed to be enough staff members in the group to interpret everyone's messages. On many occasions, a group member did not have the chance to speak out because too many others wanted to speak at the same time.

Gradually, these three women, along with the rest of the group members, acquired their own electronic aids, which produced speech output and had a visual display. They would use these aids with strangers or staff who did not know how to use the nonelectronic aids. They would also use the aids to print messages and letters.

However, they still used the nonelectronic aids with their familiar partners. In the group, they would use the electronic aids to gain attention or interrupt but, when they wanted to say something spontaneously, they would still use the nonelectronic aids, which they found to be faster.

Thus, the conversation needs of speech-impaired individuals are best served through a combination of nonelectronic and electronic aids. To provide one type of aid without the other is to provide only a partial communication system.

THE NEED FOR A NONELECTRONIC BACK-UP TO AN ELECTRONIC AID

In addition to a nonelectronic aid for use in particular situations, an individual who uses an electronic aid should always have a nonelectronic aid available as a back-up. Although most aids are durable, they will have breakdowns and malfunctions. More frequently, those in charge of maintaining the aid also will make errors resulting in the aid not working or being inaccessible to the user.

Of all the reasons for an electronic aid being unavailable to its user, inadequate charging (not charging the aid when it needs it) is probably the most frequent. Most portable electronic aids must be recharged overnight after a certain period of use; each aid varies as to how frequently it requires recharging. The aid is usually not charged because whoever is responsible for charging the aid has forgotten to do so or did not realize that this was needed. Although this can be corrected within a day by properly recharging the aid, the user will need a nonelectronic backup during the interim.

Another frequent occurrence is that the individual's caregivers have various problems that interfere with their ability to provide the aid. For example, in a large institution, a new attendant assigned to care for the individual may be unfamiliar with how to mount the aid to the wheelchair or not even know that the individual has an electronic aid. If the individual lives at home, a parent may not have had time to mount the aid to the wheelchair before the individual left for school.

A back-up is also needed when an electronic aid is not working properly and must be sent out for repairs. Usually, the aid must be repaired by the manufacturer, which may be located a long distance away, rather than by the local dealer. Repair of electronic aids, just like repair of televisions and toasters, may be delayed for any number of reasons; e.g., a special part must be ordered, or the repair person is out sick. When shipping and receiving time are added to actual repair time, it may take several weeks before the aid is returned.

In addition to the need for repairs, an aid may need to be sent to the manufacturer for a modification, such as adding speech output or changing a scanning program. As new advances in technology are made, this can be expected more frequently. Once again, as for a repair, the same shipping and receiving time are added to actual modification time.

Therefore, a problem with the functioning of the electronic aid or problems related to caregivers can prevent an individual from using the aid. These situations must be anticipated by having a nonelectronic aid available.

LEARNING ABOUT ELECTRONIC AIDS

Learning about electronic aids is a multidimensional task in which keeping current with the latest technological advances is only a small part. Even just staying current with technology can initially appear overwhelming because there are so many electronic aids to choose from and so many that appear and disappear in rapid succesion.

It is possible to become familiar with currently available aids and to keep current with new developments by reading the quarterly publications that discuss the latest developments in the field. Conferences and conventions offer an opportunity to hear other professionals discuss topics and issues in augmentative communication as well as to see many aids displayed and demonstrated. Vendors who carry electronic aids for specific geographic areas will often demonstrate equipment and may lend particular aids for a period of time. Borrowing a particular aid is an effective way of becoming familiar with it. If local vendors do not carry a particular aid, the manufacturer of the aid can be contacted to explore rental or borrowing options.

Yet, it is impossible to learn about electronic aids without learning about augmentative communication as a whole. It is essential to have some knowledge of all augmentative components, of how to evaluate particular individuals, and of how to select and implement techniques and aids for them. Some knowledge can be acquired through reading. Many articles and books have been published over the last few years that provide a basic background in augmentative communication, as well as journals that publish research and clinical studies. Assistance can also be enlisted from professionals who have developed an expertise in this area. Some may be called in as consultants to a facility or visited in facilities where they work. Developing continuing dialogues with such professionals provides a valuable source of information and learning. Local professional groups devoted to augmentative communication are a good source for meeting others involved in the field and exchanging ideas. In addition, more and more universities are offering courses in this field.

Learning about electronic communication aids also requires direct experience working with speech/writing-impaired individuals. The more practice a professional can obtain, the more he or she will learn.

Thus, there is no way to develop an expertise in electronic communication aids without learning about all augmentative means of communication and without working directly with a variety of speech/writing-impaired individuals.

REFERENCES

1. Vanderheiden, G., & Yoder, D. E. (in press). Overview. In S. W. Blackstone (Ed.), *Augmentative communication: An introduction*. Rockville, MD: American Speech and Hearing Association.
2. Salciccia, C. (1983) (unpublished letter). Request for Medicaid approval for funding of an electronic communication aid, Goldwater Memorial Hospital, New York, New York.

PART II

Determining Communication Needs

4

The Communication Needs of Speech/Writing-Impaired Individuals

THE STARTING POINT OF ASSESSMENT: COMMUNICATION NEEDS

The first objective of augmentative communication assessment is to determine the communication needs of the speech/writing-impaired individual and those he or she communicates with. Following this, a decision can be made as to which augmentative components best meet these needs. Any augmentative means of communication is useful only to the degree to which it fulfills these needs.

Communication needs fall into two broad categories: conversation and writing. Conversation needs result from the inability to produce functional speech and also may include the needs for getting attention and producing and sending messages. Writing needs result from impairment of the upper extremities. A third category to investigate is access to computers, especially for those individuals who want to pursue educational and vocational goals.

No test is commercially available that can determine all communication needs; this can only be done through direct interview and observation. Usually, this is carried out at the facility in which the speech/impaired-individual lives or attends a program or at an outpatient clinic. Those assessing the individual can be the facility's therapists, outside consultants, or both working together.

If the individual is evaluated at an outpatient clinic, it is important that significant others (therapists, family, attendants) also be present so that they can be interviewed and observed interacting with the individual. Frequently, a speech/writing-impaired individual is sent to a clinic for an evaluation without a familiar trained partner. When no significant others accompany the individual, this may indicate that they will have little time for carrying out any recommendations. In addition, if no one familiar with the individual is present, the evaluator may miss much information concerning the individual's present means of communication. Thus, the assessment should be rescheduled for a time when a significant other can also be there.

In addition to observing the speech/writing-impaired individual interact with partners, each partner and the individual should be interviewed separately. This will provide additional information that neither may want to say in front of the other. It also is a good idea for the evaluator to talk with the individual alone in order to see how effective his or her present system is with an unfamiliar partner and without an interpreter present.

Evaluators often make the mistake of considering only the environment in which the individual is evaluated and his or her position during evaluation, forgetting the need to function in other settings and positions. The result may be a communication system that the individual can use with the evaluator but with no one else.

If the evaluator needs information about functioning in other environments and direct observation is not possible, the partners must be asked specific questions about how the speech/writing-impaired individual communicates. If initially they cannot answer the questions and need to go back and observe the individual themselves, they will need an observation form with specific guidelines as to what behaviors to observe.

If the assessment is performed at the facility the speech/writing-impaired individual lives in or attends, it should include all environments in which he or she must function. Those who must communicate with the individual in each of these environments should also be interviewed to find out their needs. This is important because each environment will place different demands upon the individual. In addition, the different positions in which the individual must function in each of these environments must be considered, due to their effects on physical control. For example, an individual who is in a hospital should be observed when in bed, out of bed, in his room and outside it, receiving different therapies, during recreation, having meals, etc.

Direct observation of the speech/writing-impaired individual and partners is important, so that the evaluator can judge the individual's needs. Very often, a familiar trained partner will insist, "I understand everything he (the speech-impaired individual) says." The evaluator then observes that conversation consists of the partner asking the individual a series of yes/no questions. The individual may also have a different view of his or her communication abilities: e.g., insisting that he or she can easily communicate with everyone, when upon observation, the evaluator sees that such communication is limited to yes/no responses.

In determining needs, the future as well as the present must be considered. Communication needs change as the individual's situation changes, whether it be due to changes in physical or speech abilities (an adult with a degenerative disease) or changes in environment (a young child entering school for the first time). The needs assessment must account for these changes.

After determining the communications needs of the speech/writing-impaired individual and partners, priorities must be set. All needs will not be equally important, and often insufficient time or funds are available to fulfill all of them. Priorities should be agreed upon by the individual, the family, other familiar communication partners, and the professionals working on the case. In this way, intervention goals can be set.[1]

The attitudes of significant others will play an important part in setting priorities. Sometimes, partners will appear to agree with the evaluator's assessment of the needs although they really do not think the individual requires any specialized augmentative technique or aid. This can often be detected in the way they interact with the individual or the lack of attention they pay to the evaluator. If partners have a negative attitude toward augmentative communication — e.g., if they deny the need for augmentation or if they believe that it will be harmful to the individual — the evaluator must be aware of this.

Negative attitudes usually cannot be overcome in one session. Simply talking about it with the partners will not solve the problem. Very often, the speech/writing-impaired individual first must be trained to use an augmentative means of communication. When partners see successful results, they often become more receptive to the technique or aid.

Therefore, the first question to be asked is What does the speech/writing-impaired individual need? A needs assessment allows the individual, communication partners, and other caregivers to delineate exactly when, where, with whom, and for what purpose an augmentative communication technique will be used.[1]

COMMUNICATION NEEDS FOR PEOPLE WITH SPEECH IMPAIRMENTS

Every individual must be able to attract attention even if unable to produce voice loud enough to be heard by a partner or to produce gestures that can "catch a partner's eye." In such cases, an attention-getting device may be needed to enable the individual to call for assistance or to assist in conversation — to greet someone, to initiate a conversation, to interrupt, etc.

Attention getting is a crucial need that is often forgotten. Without the ability to gain attention for assistance, a speech-impaired individual can be at serious medical risk, because he or she may be unable to signal when in pain or danger. Without the ability to gain a partner's attention during conversation, the speech-impaired individual is unable to initiate conversation spontaneously and must depend on the approach of partners in order to communicate.

A second communication need is conversation; yet able-bodied people are often surprised at the notion that a speech-impaired individual should be able to converse. Because they may be used to seeing the individual communicate through yes/no responses or one-word utterances, it may be difficult for them to imagine that the individual is capable of expressing more or needs to do so.

An illustration of this occurred during a meeting called to plan a communication program for a 6-year-old speech/writing impaired child who needed a communication aid. The school administrator cautioned, "We should not build up his mother's hopes. After all, what could we expect this child to do?" It did not occur to the administrator that this child should be able to tell his mother what happens at school each day, answer his teacher's questions with a response more complex than yes or no, be able to share jokes with classmates, and talk about many other things that interest children his age.

A conversation between a speech-impaired individual and a partner often consists of yes/no responses to the partner's questions. Yet, conversation should be the same as for a speaking person: an exchange of ideas between two or more people on one or more topics. This includes requests and responses, but it also includes giving opinions, describing events, relating a story, asking questions, telling jokes, telling lies, cursing, etc. It includes one-word utterances, phrases, dialogues, and monologues.

Since the need for conversation takes place throughout the day, an augmentative technique or aid for conversation must be accessible to the speech-impaired individual in all situations. This may involve one means of communication or several.

A third communication need is preparing and sending messages. In this process, the speech-impaired individual prepares a message in advance to present to a partner. This method saves time by enabling the individual to initiate a topic without producing a message while the partner waits for it, at times impatiently. Messaging requires an electronic aid that will allow the individual to formulate a message, store it, and then produce it for the intended partner.[2]

COMMUNICATION NEEDS FOR PEOPLE WITH WRITING IMPAIRMENTS

As previously discussed under conversation needs, speech/writing-impaired individuals need to prepare messages on their own for later presentation to a partner. This can best be carried out through a means of writing that enables the individual to make a permanent copy of the message.

Speech/writing-impaired individuals also may need to carry out a variety of tasks that are typically carried out by able-bodied persons with a pen and paper. This includes taking class notes and exams and preparing in-class assignments, homework, and calculations. It can also include writing checks, keeping a budget, making out shopping lists, etc. These tasks all require a portable, easily accessible means of writing that can travel with the user. In addition, speech/writing-impaired individuals may also need to "write" letters, reports for school or work, manuscripts, etc., that can be carried out in one physical location, such as a desk at home, work, or school.[3]

As with conversational needs, writing needs must be determined in each environment in which the individual functions. If the individual has a means of writing, its legibility and speed should be evaluated. In addition to the writing task itself, the position and mobility of the user while performing the task are essential considerations in determining the type of writing aid required.

If the individual does not spell, it is important to determine if he or she could benefit from a means of writing. Many speech-impaired individuals never learned to spell because they could not write, but are able to learn when given a writing aid.

PARTNER LIMITATIONS

A crucial factor in the communication needs of an individual concern the limitations of partners that would interfere with their use of an augmentative means of communication. Partners include both those trained to use at least one technique or aid with the individual and those still untrained but with whom the individual would like to communicate. If a particular augmentative means of communication requires a certain ability that the partner does not have, the speech-impaired individual will not be able to communicate with that partner. Such limitations to be considered include:

Physical and sensory limitations:
> Hearing impairment (inability to respond to a buzzer or an aid producing speech output).
> Visual impairment (inability to respond to a display, print or visual selection).
> Lack of ambulation or inability to move easily into different positions (inability to use any technique or aid requiring him or her to independently change positions).
> Upper extremity involvement (inability to manipulate a piece of paper with a printed message or use a technique or device that must be held for the individual).

Cognitive and linguistic limitations:
> Inability to read (many aids requiring that the partner be able to read are provided to children, where only adults can be their communication partners, since their peers cannot read).
> Aphasia, traumatic brain injury (inability to combine individual units into a completed message).

Time limitations
Partners vary in the amount of time they can devote to communicating with a speech-impaired individual. Volunteers and friends may have more time to devote than professionals who are preoccupied with providing services to many clients or a parent with many children to care for. If a partner with whom the individual must converse frequently has limited time, then an augmentative means of communication probably will not be used if it requires a significant period of time for either learning or communicating with the individual.

ESTABLISHING INITIAL INTERACTION MECHANISMS IN ORDER TO ASSESS NEEDS

Individuals come to the communication needs assessment with whatever augmentative means of communication they are presently using. These means will vary widely in the degree to which an untrained partner can understand them. Some individuals use techniques or aids that are intelligible to strangers without any prior training (such as aids producing speech output). Other people have developed elaborate means to interact with familiar trained persons — eyes looking up means yes; a protruding tongue means "I'm hungry"; an eye blink means "I'm tired" — but are unable to interact with an untrained person without an interpreter. Many others have not yet developed effective means of interacting with anyone, especially if the speech impairment is recent.

Where a speech-impaired individual is unable to interact with the evaluator or caregivers, an initial interaction mechanism must be established. The more severe the speech and physical impairment, the less standard augmentative techniques the individual will be able to use and the more a special technique or aid will have to be developed.

In establishing initial interaction mechanisms, first evaluate the individual's awareness of his or her surroundings and general understanding of what is happening; (For instance, does he or she attend to the evaluator? look at items that are referred to? respond to humorous remarks?)

Second, establish that the individual demonstrates a desire to interact, e.g., tries to initiate communication through vocalization, facial expression, or body movements.

Third, locate a consistent physical movement that the individual can produce upon request, e.g., "Move your thumb," "Look up." If initially not able to produce a consistent movement, the individual may need repositioning; e.g., may have more physical ability when sitting up than when supine. Care must be taken that the movement is performed upon request and not as a reflex response or random movement.

Once it is determined that the individual can produce a movement consistently upon request, it must be determined whether the movement can be used as an indicator of choices presented to him or her. Initially, it is important to present several choices, rather than ask the individual to make a choice from only two items, so that there is more than a 50 percent chance that the response is not random.

The best way to test whether a movement can be used as an indicator is if the evaluator does not know the answer to the question. This requires the presence of a second person who is familiar with the individual to give the evaluator a question to ask that the individual can answer.

For example, suppose the individual is a child who can respond by raising her eyebrows. The child receives home tutoring on Tuesday and Thursday. Her mother, who knows that the child knows this information, tells the evaluator to ask her what days the tutor comes to her house. The evaluator then proceeds to name each day of the week. The child responds when the days that the tutor comes are named. The evaluator can then verify his or her understanding of the individual's response with the familiar partner.

Fourth, when the individual appears able to use a consistent movement to indicate, then attempt to use this indicator to find out more information about the individual and his or her needs. When presenting such questions, it is important to phrase them so they can be answered with a yes or no. For example, it would be impossible to answer the question, What did you do this weekend? with a yes or no. The question must be broken down into several more specific questions, as follows:

Did you go away this weekend?
Did you visit someone?
Did you go someplace outside?

If the individual does not respond or is inconsistent in the responses, care must be taken that other factors, such as sensory impairments, are not interfering. For example, caution should be used in presenting visual materials unless the individual can indicate whether the materials can be seen. An undetected hearing problem also can produce misleading results.

Many severely disabled individuals who have recently become speech impaired are depressed or immediately reject anyone who tries to help them. This behavior should not be confused with other impairments.

Severely physically disabled individuals, whether the condition is recently acquired or has gone on for years, often do not respond well in new environments and may need to become more familiar with their surroundings before they can adequately demonstrate their abilities. An individual who is not responding during the initial evaluation should be observed with more familiar persons, and if possible, reevaluated over a period of time.

Establishing an interaction mechanism with a child often requires a different approach than with an adult. Many children will not respond to a task (e.g., "Raise your eyebrows") but will respond to a game or activity that interests them.

These are meant to be general guidelines to establish an initial interaction mechanism with a severely speech-impaired individual, who may have limited ability to use standard augmentative techniques. Once established, this mechanism can then be used to further determine the individual's communication needs.

REFERENCES

1. Beukelman, D. R., Yorkston, K. M., & Dowden, P. A. (1985). *Communication augmentation: A casebook of clinical management* (p. 9) San Diego, CA: College-Hill Press.
2. Vanderheiden, G. (1983). Nonconversational communication technology needs of individuals with handicaps. *Rehabilitation World*, 7, 9.
3. Vanderheiden, P. J. (1985). Writing aids. In J. G. Webster et al. (Eds.), *Electronic devices for rehabilitation* (p. 264). New York: John Wiley & Sons

5

Evaluating Augmentative Components: Ten Crucial Dimensions Used to Evaluate Components

Many dimensions can be used to evaluate an augmentative technique, a symbol set, or the features of a communication aid. Some dimensions can be used to evaluate several components, while others apply only to one. These dimensions can be used to assess the effectiveness of the augmentative components that comprise the individual's present communication system, to compare components, and to determine which components will best meet this individual's communication needs. For a complete description of all dimensions, the reader is referred to Vanderheiden and Lloyd.[1]

Ten important dimensions to be assessed are described. These dimensions also will be used throughout the book to evaluate the components and features implemented through a communication aid.

INTELLIGIBILITY OF MESSAGES

The intelligibility of messages is determined by the obviousness of the components used. A component that is obvious does not require prior training before a partner can understand it. The more obvious a component is, the greater are the number of people with whom the individual can communicate. For example, direct selection is a more obvious technique than scanning. Letters of the alphabet are more obvious symbols to a greater number of people than pictographs.[1]

The output of an electronic communication aid also can be evaluated in terms of the obviousness of the messages it produces. Messages produced through speech output are highly obvious, while messages produced through print are obvious to those who can read.

If the individual is using an augmentative selection technique or symbol system that is not obvious, the intelligibility of the message will depend upon the familiarity of the communication partner both to the components and to the individual using them. This can vary with each partner. For example, a mother may know that one type of sound her son produces means he needs help. She may also understand a great deal of what her son says through his speech. However, the child's teacher may not be able to distinguish when he needs help from the other sounds he makes and may be unable to understand anything he tries to say through his speech. While the son's means of communication are intelligible to his mother, they are not to his teacher. Thus, the determination that an individual's communication is intelligible must be made in relation to how well each partner understands him or her.

In addition to obviousness, intelligibility also depends upon the individual's ability to add emotional emphasis to the text of a message. Paralinguistic aspects of speech, such as rate, stress, pauses, and intonation, used by able-bodied persons to convey a particular meaning or to clarify a communication, may be unavailable to the speech-impaired person. This may create misunderstandings or may make meaning ambiguous; e.g., humor or sarcasm may not be understood.[2]

If the individual has a means of writing, it, too should be evaluated in terms of its ability to allow production of legible messages.

RATE OF MESSAGE PRODUCTION

This dimension is used to evaluate the speed with which an augmentative selection technique can be used to send messages. There is a very large gap between the conversation rate of able-bodied speakers and that of speech-impaired individuals using augmentative techniques. Conversation between able-bodied speakers takes place at the rate of about 180-200 wpm (words per minnute). Augmentative communication rates reported in the literature range from 2-26 wpm[2]. These figures were obtained primarily from individuals using alphabet arrays with direct selection and row-column scanning techniques. Use of whole words and prediction of messages from several letters or words can increase rate of communication. However, the overall rate of communication for a speech-impaired individual using an augmentative technique remains considerably below that of speech.

This large gap in conversation rate gives the able-bodied partner a natural advantage and dominance over the speech-impaired individual, which determines what the individual can do and say effectively and efficiently.[2] It also determines which techniques will be preferred by partners and speech-impaired individuals. In general, the techniques that can be used most rapidly will be preferred over those that produce messages at a slower rate, regardless of whether the technique or the aid attains high ratings in other dimensions.

Writing rate is also important; especially, if the individual must compete with able-bodied peers in school or at work. Able-bodied persons can write at about 30-35 wpm, so that the difference between the performance of able-bodied and writing-impaired persons in writing is much less than in conversation.[3]

ASSERTABILITY

Assertability is the ability to interrupt, to resist interruptions, and to maintain conversational control, including obtaining and maintaining speaking turns, initiating topics, and changing from responder to initiator.[4] Able-bodied speakers maintain this control through supplying each other continuous feedback through standard techniques, such as gestures, eye contact, facial expression, nodding, and saying "yes," "sure," etc.

Physical disability may limit the ability of speech-impaired individuals to supply continuous feedback through standard techniques. A communication aid can add or detract to this dimension depending upon its output. For example, continuous feedback can be supplied to the partner through a visual display that shows the letters of a message as it is being produced. It can also be produced through the echo function of a speech output aid, which will produce each word aloud as the individual selects it.

INDEPENDENCE IN PRODUCING MESSAGES

If the individual needs a familiar partner in order to produce messages or to translate them or if there are times when the individual is left unable to communicate because no assistant is available, then the individual is highly dependent.[1] The individual's independence also is influenced by mobility. A person who cannot move independently may be more dependent on a partner's independent approach in order to communicate than one who could approach a partner when necessary.

Independence is as important in writing as it is in conversation. Without the ability to write independently, an individual may be dependent on a scribe to write for him or her, limiting the ability to effectively participate in educational or vocational activities.

ABILITY TO PROJECT

A technique or aid may need to be used at a distance from a partner.[1] If a speech-impaired individual can only communicate with a partner when they are in close physical proximity or if the partner is unable to engage in other activities while communicating with the individual, then the aid or technique is limited in projection. An inability to project also will prevent the individual from communicating with a partner who is not positioned close enough to see the individual's selection display.

The farther away are the speech-impaired individual and the partner, the more the individual needs to project, since the partner may not be able to see the individual or any technique that is used. This includes communicating in groups, in a classroom, in front of an audience, or over the phone.

The lighting and acoustics of the environment also influence the ability to project. In one environment, individuals may be able to gain attention through their voices or to converse through speech and gestures but be unable to do so in a noisier or less well lit location.

DISPLAY PERMANENCE

A presentation can be temporary, such as speech, signs, or symbols selected on a nonelectronic aid. It can be an erasable sentence, such as words on an electronic visual display or a permanently printed display.[1] Display permanence is crucial for writing needs, where the user is able to prepare material in advance of presenting it. It is also important for conversation, where it allows the partner to see a message as it is being produced instead of having to wait for the entire message to be presented.

The ability to display a message affects other dimensions of an overall communication system. The ability to accumulate letters can increase communication rate by eliminating the need to wait for the partner to register each element as it is indicated and by allowing the message to be predicted before it is complete. A visual display can improve the individual's ability to maintain conversational control by providing continuous feedback to the partner as the individual formulates a message. The display improves intelligibility by giving the user access to words not on the selection display, by putting up a number of clues that the partner can study. Feedback provided to the user also facilitates growth and learning.[1]

CORRECTABILITY OF MESSAGES

The ability to unambiguously repair or correct utterances is important in both writing and conversation. Correctability is best provided through a visible correctable display, although it also can be provided through techniques not using a display, such as signing, where the individual can correct mistakes more easily because he or she produces the signs. Correctability is most difficult to accomplish with nondisplay-based techniques that are partner-dominated, such as scanning with a nonelectronic aid, where the partner indicates each item for the individual.[1] This usually results in the partner interpreting the communication as well as anticipating, often incorrectly, the individual's words or intentions.

Correctability is very important in terms of improving the intelligibility of messages, motivation to use a technique, and accurate assessment of an individual's abilities. With regard to motivation, disabled users very much want their output to be correct, to represent their true abilities, and to transfer the exact content of a message to their partner. With regard to assessment, the correctable display allows errors due to physical or other factors to be separated from errors due to misunderstanding.[1]

ACCESSIBILITY

This refers to the ability of the technique or aid to be available to the user when he needs it. One factor that determines accessibility is the ability of the individual to use the technique or aid independently.[1] A second factor is the portability of an aid. An aid that can be carried with an individual will be more accessible than one that must be used in a single location. The individual who must be brought an aid before being able to say or write something has far less access to communication than if the aid were mounted where it could be used at will. The positioning requirements for use of a selection technique also affects its accessibility. A technique that can only be used when the individual is in a particular position is less accessible than a technique that can be used regardless of the individual's position.

OPENNESS/EXPANDABILITY

Openness refers to the ability of a symbol system to represent the thoughts the individual wants to express. For example, the alphabet is an open system, because an individual can express any word he or she wants and can spell. Openness also refers to the ability of a technique or aid to allow production, display, or storage of vocabulary items the individual wants to express. For example, the openness of American Sign Language is only limited by the number of signs the individual can produce, while the openness of a nonelectronic aid may be limited by the number of spaces available to display items.

Expandability refers to the ability of the technique to expand easily to accommodate the addition of new vocabulary items or new ways to use existing vocabulary. For example, a communication board with no space to add new items would have very limited expandability, while a programmable electronic aid with a large memory in which to store items has great expandability.[1]

FLEXIBILITY

This allows the technique or aid to be modified to meet a particular individual's needs and abilities. For example, a nonelectronic aid that can be custom-designed for an individual's physical abilities is more flexible than an electronic aid that only can be controlled through direct selection.

Flexibility also refers to the ability of the aid or technique to be modified as an individual's needs or abilities change. For example, a child just entering school will need to write as well as to have conversations. His aid should be able to provide for that additional need. An individual with a degenerative condition may be able to use direct selection at the onset of the condition but may later need an aid controlled through scanning as his condition progresses.

In addition, flexibility includes the ability of the aid to be easily mounted, unmounted, and transported without a great deal of difficulty.[1]

EXAMPLE: A COMMUNICATION NEEDS ASSESSMENT

The following example shows how communication needs can be determined by evaluating the components of an individual's overall communication system.

Mrs. Harris, a 68-year-old woman, was diagnosed as having ALS six years ago. Within the last year, she lost the ability to speak intelligibly, although she can still produce a barely audible voice. Mrs. Harris is able to write legibly, although very slowly. She communicates primarily through vocalizations, gestures, facial expressions, and writing.

Mrs. Harris is able to walk with the assistance of a walker. However, most of the day she sits in a wheelchair in the living room, as she is unable to move the chair independently.

Mrs. Harris lives alone and is cared for by 24-hour private nurses, who are the primary people she needs to speak with. Friends come to visit her once a week. Mrs. Harris also needs to speak over the phone with her children and grandchildren, who live in various parts of the country.

Mrs. Harris is able to gain the attention of her nurse by vocalizing when one of them is in the room with her. However, when she is in a different room, Mrs. Harris has no way to call for assistance. At one point, she had an intercom system but is no longer able to push the buttons to operate it nor to speak into it.

Conversation with her nurses is carried out basically through vocalizing and gestures. Most conversation consists of the nurse asking Mrs. Harris yes/no questions. When the nurse cannot guess, Mrs. Harris writes her message, which usually consists of one or two words. Writing is legible but slow. Mrs. Harris uses the same techniques with her visitors, who need the assistance of the nurses in order to understand her.

In addition to conversation/messaging, Mrs. Harris also has writing needs. She is still quite active in her occupation, appraising Spanish American art, and collectors continue to send pieces to her. Currently, she writes her appraisals in longhand, as she no longer is able to use a typewriter.

Since Mrs. Harris has a degenerative disease which has progressed more rapidly in the past year, her speech and writing abilities can be expected to further deteriorate, although the rate of progression cannot be certain.

The components of Mrs. Harris's present overall communication system can be evaluated along the following dimensions described in this chapter:

- *Intelligibility of messages:* This is limited primarily to the nurses. Strangers and those who know Mrs. Harris but have less experience in communicating with her require a nurse to interpret what she is saying.
- *Rate:* Conversation rate is very slow, so that most of the time conversation is limited to yes/no questions and one word messages. Writing also is very slow.
- *Assertability*: Due to her reduced vocal loudness and gestural ability, there is no effective method for Mrs. Harris to interrupt during a conversation or to avoid being interrupted.

- *Independence*: Unless she writes a message, Mrs. Harris is very dependent on the nurses to produce a message or to talk to anyone else.
- *Projection*: There is no method for Mrs. Harris to project when she is at a distance from the nurses nor can she communicate over the phone.
- *Display permanence and correctability*: Writing provides Mrs. Harris with a permanent display and is somewhat correctable, but it is becoming laborious and inefficient for her. She cannot produce written material of high quality because of limited editing ability.
- *Flexibility*: As her physical condition progresses, there will be no means to adapt the techniques that Mrs. Harris presently uses.

Mrs. Harris's priority is an augmentative means of communication for conversations held face to face and over the phone. She does not see the need for a writing aid because she feels that she can still write her reports and messages adequately in longhand and has no other need for writing. Even though she says that she is aware of the progressive nature of her condition, Mrs. Harris does not appear to understand that she will probably lose the ability to write or to produce sounds altogether.

The priority for both the nurses and Mrs. Harris's family is a way for her to call for assistance. The nurses would also like a faster method of conversation, while the family would like to speak to Mrs. Harris directly over the phone.

From this assessment, the following needs were decided upon by Mrs. Harris and her primary communication partners:

1. Gaining attention when a partner is at a distance.
2. Speaking over the phone independently.
3. When speech and gesture are not intelligible to nurses, augmenting face-to-face conversation through a faster, less tiring technique than writing in longhand.
4. Preparing messages in advance through a faster, less tiring technique than writing in longhand.

In addition, Mrs. Harris will also need a means of writing formal reports and correspondence in the future, although she does not consider this to be a priority.

Since Mrs. Harris's physical and speech abilities are extremely limited, and she is making use of standard augmentative techniques as fully as possible, the next step is to investigate various communication aids that can meet Mrs. Harris's needs.

REFERENCES

1. Vanderheiden, G., & Lloyd, L. (in press), Communication systems and their components. In S. W. Blackstone (Ed.), *Augmentative communication: An introduction*. Rockville, MD: American Speech and Hearing Association.

2. Kraat, A. W. (in press). Developing appropriate intervention goals. In S.W. Blackstone (Ed.), *Augmentative communication: An introduction*. Rockville, MD: American Speech and Hearing Association.

3. Vanderheiden, G. (1983). Non-conversational communication technology needs of individuals with handicaps, *Rehabilitation World, 7*, 11.

4. Farrier, L. D., Yorkston, K. M., Marriner, N. A., & Beukelman, D. R. (1985). Conversational control in nonimpaired speakers using an augmentative communication system. *Augmentative and Alternative Communication, 1*, 65.

PART III

The Output of Communication Aids

The outputs of electronic aids are going through a period of rapid development. Practically every month, a more intelligible synthesizer, a more portable printer, or a larger visual display is introduced, making it seem as if no final decision can be made to select one form of output over another.

Despite the changes in the quality, size, shape, and even cost of output devices, the basic types of output and the communication needs they meet remain the same. Each form of output is more effective in providing certain dimensions of conversation than others. It is necessary to understand the differences among their capabilities so that the most effective form of output is selected to fill the speech/writing-impaired individual's needs in a particular situation.

As discussed in Chapter 1, there are five types of output: attention-getters, visual selection (nonelectronic and electronic), speech, visual display, and print. While an aid that visually selects items or produces speech output can be used for conversation, one with a visual display and a printer can be used for conversation, messaging, and writing needs. All aids can have an attention-getting call signal as part of the aid or physically separate from it.

The ability of each form of output to meet these needs can be evaluated along the dimensions discussed in Chapter 5:

Intelligibility of messages
Rate of communication
Ability to produce messages independently
Assertability; ability to maintain conversational control
Projection
Display permanence
Correctability

Most individuals will need access to several forms of output and will use different types for different needs and with different partners. One output is only "better" than another in terms of meeting the needs of a specific situation, but in most cases, no one output can meet all the needs of an individual.

6

Attention-Getters

TYPES OF ATTENTION-GETTERS

An attention-getter is a type of auditory output that is sufficiently loud and distinctive to be heard over the rest of the noise in the environment. It can be part of a communication aid or environmental control unit, or it can be physically separate, such as a buzzer. Even if an aid includes an attention-getting device, the individual will usually still need a separate attention-getter for those times when the aid is not available.

Attention-getters that are separate from aids include whistles, bells, or any other devices the individual can activate and that are loud enough to be heard. Buzzers, purchased commercially or homemade, can be designed to meet different physical abilities. Some, designed for those who must use a single switch, can be activated using the same switch and control site that an individual uses to operate the communication aid (Fig. 6–1). Some are designed for individuals with good fine-motor movement, who can activate a switch with their hands or fingers (Fig. 6-2).

Attention-getters that are part of communication aids or environmental control units usually produce some type of alarm or noise. The individual activates the attention-getter by selecting the appropriate target on the aid's selection display. With some aids, the alarm goes off automatically after a period of time, while with others, the alarm does not go off until someone shuts it off.

EVALUATING ATTENTION-GETTERS

At any time when a partner is not paying visual attention to the individual, whether in another room or sitting nearby, the individual needs some way to gain attention. Thus, an attention-getting device can be evaluated as to how well it allows an individual to project; i.e., communicate with someone at a distance. The distance a device can project depends upon the volume of noise that it produces. The louder the noise, the greater the projection. A device that is too loud, however, can be annoying. For example, in a classroom, a buzzer should enable a student to gain the teacher's attention but should not be so loud that the teacher wants to disconnect it. Another consideration is the distinctiveness of the noise produced. The attention-getter should

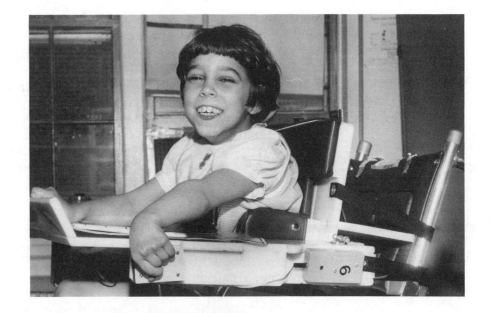

FIGURE 6.1 A child activating a switch connected to a buzzer. The switch, mounted to the side of a laptray, is activated with her hand. (Photo by Corbit's Studio, Bridgeport, CT. Buzzer and switch by Arroyo and Associates, Glendale, NY.)

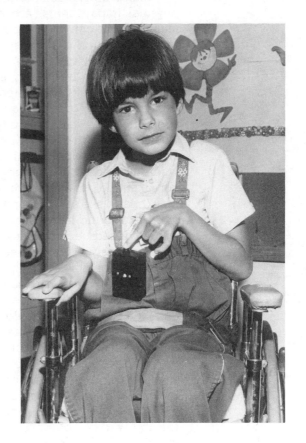

FIGURE 6.2 A child with a buzzer clipped onto his clothing. By pressing the small switch mounted on the buzzer, the child activates it. (Photo by Corbit's Studio. Buzzer by Mark Cavanna, Cerebral Palsy Center, Bridgeport, CT.)

produce a sound that is distinctive from other sounds in the environment, e.g., on a respiratory ward, the nurses must be able to distinguish the sound of the attention-getter from the sounds of the respirators.

Depending on the different environments in which the individual must function, more than one attention-getting device may be needed; e.g., a device to be used at night, to gain the attention of those who are in another room and who may be sleeping, produces one level and type of sound; another device to be used to interrupt and initiate conversation when a partner is in closer proximity, requires a lower volume and different quality of sound.

WHO NEEDS AN ATTENTION-GETTER?

In many cases, it is clear when an individual needs an attention-getting device, e.g., an individual who cannot produce any voice and who is not mobile. Even when in close proximity, attendants cannot always pay visual attention to the individual, who needs some way to gain their attention at certain times.

Many individuals, even though they have severe speech and physical impairments, are able to gain attention through unaided means. Some can click their tongues, others can vocalize loudly, etc. In each situation, a judgment must be made as to whether the unaided means is adequate.

A problem frequently arises as to whether an attention-getting device is needed with speech-impaired cerebral palsied children in a classroom or group. Many of these children can laugh, cry, and spontaneously vocalize quite loudly to express various emotions. It would appear that they would be able to call for attention as well. However, many of these children have difficulty initiating vocalizations when they need to, although they can spontaneously produce them. For example, a teacher reported that, on turning around from the blackboard, she saw that one of the children in her class was struggling to make a sound to get her attention but nothing would come out. She was surprised because the same child could make a variety of sounds spontaneously. She also had no idea of how long the child had been struggling or how often this had gone on without her noticing it.

A question often arises as to whether an individual who has no means of communicating except through vocalizations, eye pointing, and facial expression should be given an attention-getting device. This may occur with individuals who have not yet been given other specialized augmentative means of communication, either because they are still being evaluated or there is some difficulty in doing so; e.g., a problem with attending or with recognizing pictographs. If such an individual is unable to gain attention through unaided techniques, the attention-getter should probably be the first thing he is given, since the ability to call others over and to gain control of one's environment is crucial to the development of interaction and communication.

Thus, an individual who is unable to gain attention through unaided techniques should be given an attention-getting device. The need for this device must be evaluated in each situation and with each of the individual's communication partners.

"MISBEHAVING" WITH AN ATTENTION-GETTER

For many speech-impaired children, an attention-getting device enables them to exert control over their surroundings for the first time. As a result, many will use it when they do not really need help but would just like to "play a joke." Others may continuously activate the buzzer. These behaviors usually last for only a short while, until the novelty of the device has diminished. The best way to handle the situation is to treat the behavior as if the child were able to speak; i.e., through whatever reprimands are taken for any child who continuously makes noise. Disconnecting the device or taking it away is similar to putting tape over a child's mouth, so this course of action should be avoided.

A similar situation can arise with adults whose severe speech and physical impairments are acquired conditions. An individual may constantly activate a buzzer to call for assistance or to initiate a conversation, which may become annoying to the partner who is called. This situation should also be treated as if the individual were calling the partner or attendant through his speech. Removing the device will alleviate the annoying sound for the partner, but it will not solve the individual's problem, whether a need for attention, a need to exert some control over the environment, or a real physical discomfort that cannot be easily resolved.

7

Visual Selection

EVALUATING NONELECTRONIC VISUAL SELECTION IN MEETING COMMUNICATION NEEDS

When using a nonelectronic aid, the speech-impaired individual indicates an item from a display directly to the partner through one of several selection techniques. Although the aid does not produce any output, for the sake of comparison with electronic aids, this can be called *nonelectronic visual selection*.

The most effective way to demonstrate visual selection is with an illustration and an example of a dialogue. Figure 7-1 shows a speech-impaired individual and partner in a typical position for conversation. The partner is in close proximity to the individual and, in this case, must watch the individual as she directly points to an item on her nonelectronic aid display. The individual is using a communication aid consisting of pictographs, whole words, and phrases. The conversation might proceed as follows:

> *Partner:* What are you doing next week?
> *Child:* (pointing to items on her board) Mommy.
> *Partner:* (saying the item aloud as the child indicates it) Mommy.
> *Child:* Daddy.
> *Partner:* Daddy.
> *Child:* Me.
> *Partner:* Me. OK, Mommy, Daddy, and you.
> *Child:* (nodding to indicate partner is correct so far) Go.
> *Partner:* Go.
> *Child:* Vacation.
> *Partner:* Vacation. Oh, you and your parents are going on a vacation. Is that right?
> *Child:* (Nods to indicate the partner is correct.)
> *Partner:* Oh, how nice!

Although this may seem slow and laborious and poses many limitations for the user, nonelectronic visual selection rates high in meeting conversation needs in several important dimensions: assertability, rate, and ability to express emotional emphasis.

Assertability

The user is able to exert greater conversational control than with many electronic aids. The partner's attention to the individual's indications and interpretation of messages take the place of continuous feedback supplied by able-bodied speakers conversing with each other.

Rate

Communication rates for individuals using nonelectronic aids vary greatly, mostly depending upon whether they are communicating a commonly known, highly predictable sentence, and the degree of familiarity of the partner with the selection technique the individual is using. The partner also may be able to predict the message from a few words or letters. If the partner needs only two letters to guess a word and two words to guess a sentence, the effective word per minute rate increases.[1]

Independence

Throughout the visual selection process, the partner must devote full attention to the individual, and what he or she is selecting. If the partner turns away, even for a second, the user is silenced during that time.

The individual is totally dependent on the partner's presence to produce and present a message. No communication can be prepared in advance. The partner must interpret each item, usually by saying it aloud so that the individual can confirm or deny its correctness and then combine the items to form a message.

Projection

The partner must be in close physical proximity to the individual in order to see the aid's selection display and the items that he or she selects.

Intelligibility

This dimension rates low because the use of many nonelectronic aids are not obvious to strangers and require extensive partner training before use. The partner must learn how items are indicated, when a new word starts, when a mistake is made, when the individual wants to continue or finish, whether the message can be predicted or must be completed, and many other procedures that enable a conversation to take place rapidly.

Becoming proficient in the use of a nonelectronic aid with an individual takes time, time that many people do not have. Very often, the only persons who know how to use the nonelectronic aid are the professionals assigned to the individual's case. As a result, few people may actually be able to communicate with the user of a nonelectronic aid.

Intelligibility also is limited because the partner is responsible for interpreting items. This limits use of the aid to those who understand the symbol set used with the aid. For example, a young child who cannot read or spell will not be able to understand the items indicated by an individual who uses spelling. A stranger will usually not be able to understand a symbol set that is not obvious, such as pictographs.

Correctability

Because the partner is responsible for interpreting the message, it is difficult for the user to transfer exact content or to communicate exactly what he wants to say without the partner's embellishment or interpretation. It may also be difficult for the user to correct a partner who has so much of the communication process under his control.

Display Permanence

The items the individual selects to form a message are displayed permanently (either written or drawn), but no display pieces them together as they are selected. This puts a burden on the partner and the user, who must remember each item as it is selected. As a result, nonelectronic aid users can easily repeat themselves or form confused messages. A strategy that can assist both partner and user is for the partner to write down each item the user selects for later study if there is trouble interpreting the message.

Thus, nonelectronic aids are more effective to use in certain situations more than in others, and with certain partners more than with others.

UNDERSTANDING AND RATING ELECTRONIC VISUAL SELECTION

An electronic visual selection aid indicates an item directly to the partner through a light or a rotating arrow.[2] The item is selected by the user through linear or row-column scanning. This is in contrast to visual selection with a nonelectronic aid, where the individual indicates the item by direct selection or the partner scans each item until the individual indicates the desired item through a prearranged signal (Fig. 7-2).

FIGURE 7.2 The Dial-Scan, an electronic visual selection aid controlled with a single switch. (Drawing courtesy of Don Johnston Development Equipment, Inc., Lake Zurich, IL.)

These aids may be custom-made or commercially available. Some have additional memories that allow the user to store a certain number of vocabulary items, which can be recalled when the partner is present. For example, the ZYGO 100, a scanning visual selection aid, has a memory that can store up to 16 items. When recalled, the aid will automatically indicate the items in the sequence in which they were stored.

Electronic visual selection rates higher than nonelectronic visual selection in certain dimensions. The individual is more independent because of the ease in initiating communication. Messages can be prepared in advance if the aid has a memory. Strangers and untrained partners may find it easier to understand a message output because they do not have to indicate items for the individual. Aids with large selection displays can be seen at a distance, so that the user and partner do not have to be in close proximity. Some devices have an indicator on both sides of the display for viewing in a more natural position for conversation.

However, electronic visual selection has most of the limitations of nonelectronic visual selection: the partner must still piece together a message, be present to receive the message, understand the symbol set used, etc. It also has the same limitations of vocabulary openness, because the individual is limited to the number of items that can be printed or drawn on the aid's selection display. In addition, since it is controlled through scanning, the communication rate is usually slower than can be achieved with a nonelectronic scanning aid.

USES AND MISUSES OF ELECTRONIC VISUAL SELECTION AIDS

Despite their limitations, electronic visual selection aids can be effectively used in several ways. One of these is for assessing or training in scanning and switch control. These aids give an individual specific targets to aim for, as well as feedback, through the indicator, of the accuracy of the selection. If the vocabulary items that the individual wants to communicate or select are placed in these targets, the task becomes more functional and motivating. For example, a game can be played in which the individual must direct someone to move forward, backward, left, or right through selecting items.

Another use is as a supplement to a nonelectronic aid. A nonelectronic scanning or encoding aid used with a pictographic system will require extensive partner training. An individual with this type of nonelectronic aid and no electronic aid may lack partners willing or trained to use the aid. Also, communication with strangers is curtailed. For example, a speech-impaired child in a hospital for a short stay must work with staff members who do not know his or her communication modes. An electronic visual selection aid can provide the child with the ability to communicate crucial items that could not be communicated otherwise. However, an individual who is given an electronic visual selection aid without a nonelectronic aid is limited to the small number of items the aid displays and can indicate items only through scanning. For face-to-face conversation with familiar partners, conversation using a nonelectronic aid with a scanning technique usually is faster.

Frequently, an individual is given a visual selection aid because it is considered easier to control a switch than to select items with a nonelectronic aid. However, an individual who has the ability to control a switch has consistent physical movement, which can be used as an indicator with nonelectronic scanning.

REFERENCES

1. Vanderheiden, G. (1984). Personal communication.
2. Kraat, A. W. (1982). Output modes available in communication devices. Paper presented at Communication Aids Workshop, West Lake, OH.

8

Speech Output

WHY SPEECH SYNTHESIS IS USED WITH COMMUNICATION AIDS

Many professionals, family members, and speech-impaired individuals do not like the sound of speech output aids. The most common complaints are that they sound too mechanical or artificial or that they cannot be understood.

The type of speech output used with communication aids is usually synthesized speech, which is produced artificially through a speech synthesizer. A synthesizer is a machine that talks according to programmed instructions rather than playing back previously recorded speech. Because the synthesizer creates its speech output, it must be able to imitate all the characteristics of the speech mechanism. Trying to do this electronically is extremely difficult, with the result that speech synthesis often sounds unnatural and may have limited intelligibility.[1]

In contrast, digitized speech, which uses human speech as its basis and digitally records it, can be more intelligible and natural-sounding than synthesized speech, but it is more expensive because it uses a large amount of memory. Also, the vocabulary of the system is limited to prestored words.[2]

The advantages of speech synthesis are that it does not require a large memory, so its cost can be kept low, and any item can be rapidly and easily constructed. However, it is less natural sounding or intelligible than many speech-impaired individuals and their partners would like it to be.[1]

Different synthesizers are used with computer-based and dedicated communication aids, depending upon the preference of the manufacturer. Synthesizers also can be purchased separately for use with microcomputers.

EVALUATING SPEECH OUTPUT

Speech output rates high in projection and the ability to gain attention, to interrupt, and to resist interruptions. Speech output's rating in intelligibility depends upon several factors. One is the intelligibility of the particular synthesizer being used. Another aspect, as discussed in the next section, is the ability of the user to manipulate the variables of the synthesizer to make speech more intelligible. The ability to add emotional emphasis, which depends upon whether the individual can control inflection, pausing, volume, and pitch changes of the particular synthesizer, also influences intelligibility. A third aspect is the ability of the partners to be trained to understand the particular speech output produced by the aid.

When speech output is intelligible, it eliminates the need for the partner to understand the symbol set that the individual is using. It also increases the user's independence because the partner does not have to interpret the message as the individual produces it; instead, the entire message is presented to the partner without need for participation. This means that the individual's communication is understood by a greater number of partners and the number of potential partners an individual can have is increased. It also allows communication with those who have visual or cognitive/linguistic impairments (who cannot read, spell, or understand a particular symbol set).

Although speech synthesis occurs at approximately the same rate as speech, the programming of the message takes as long as if the aid were printing out the message. It takes approximately the same number of phonemes to program a synthesizer to speak a message as it does letters to spell out a message. Even with prestored phrases, there still can be a long period between selection and expression of the phrase, depending upon the selection technique used.[1]

The need for the partner to wait for the message affects the user's ability to maintain conversational control. This can be illustrated by an example of what a conversation using speech output might be like:

> *Partner:*   What are you doing next week? (Anywhere from several seconds to several minutes passes as the user constructs his message.)
> *User:*   (using speech output)   Mommy, Daddy, and me are going on a vacation.
> *Partner:*   Oh, how nice!

Since there is no need for the partner to interpret the message and no continuous feedback as the individual constructs the message (except by looking over the individual's shoulder, to see what he or she is selecting), the partner must wait for the user to produce the entire message before hearing it. During the long silence (depending upon the control technique used and the physical ability of the user) as the user constructs the message, there is plenty of time for the partner to ask another question, interrupt message preparation with a series of questions in an attempt to accelerate the conversation, change the subject, start talking to someone else, or even walk away.

Because there is no continuous feedback, there is also no opportunity for the partner to predict the message and increase the rate of message production. This is alleviated somewhat when the aid has an echo feature, which allows each item to be spoken as it is selected.

If an aid with speech output also has a visual display and the partner is in close enough proximity to see it, the partner may often look at the display rather than listen to the speech. This may be due to the limited intelligibility of the particular synthesizer. It also may be due to the need for some type of feedback while the partner waits for a message. The display also helps the partner to predict the message before it is completed, which increases communication rate.

Thus, a conversation with an individual using an aid that produces only speech output will be much slower than normal speech. As a result, familiar partners may prefer to use the individual's nonelectronic aid or an electronic aid with a visual display. Speech output then is reserved for communicating at a distance; for those who have visual, physical, or cognitive impairments or other limitations preventing them from understanding other forms of output; and for those who are unfamiliar with less obvious techniques and aids the individual uses.

Speech output rates low in display permanence. A message produced through a speech output aid is temporary. If a message is not understood, it can be repeated, but there is no way for a partner to spend time trying to decipher it after it has been spoken.

A programmable speech output aid has some application for messaging in that messages can be prepared in advance, stored, and then presented to a partner. Unlike printing a message on paper, the aid and user both must be present to produce a message through speech output.

Most programmable aids enable the user to correct a message that is prepared in advance and stored for later presentation by constructing the message, producing it through speech output, and then correcting it if necessary. It may be more difficult to effectively correct messages constructed during spontaneous, face-to-face conversation, rather than items that are prestored. Because of the lack of display permanence, speech output cannot be used for any writing needs.

CONSIDERATIONS IN SELECTING SPEECH OUTPUT

● **Can the Intelligibility of the Synthesizer Be Increased?**

A particular synthesizer may seem unintelligible until its user learns how to adequately manipulate its variables. This was one of the implications of a study conducted by Kraat and Levinson (1984) that investigated the intelligibility of two popular synthesizers used with communication aids, the Echo II and the Votrax Personal Speech System (PSS).

These two synthesizer systems were compared for intelligibility on an eight-word sentence task presented to 20 adult listeners in two modes of presentation: as a full sentence spoken at a normal rate and as a sentence with $2\frac{1}{2}$-second pauses between words. The results of the study indicated that the Votrax PSS was the superior system when the sentence was presented without pauses. With pauses, intelligibility was improved for both synthesizers, and the intelligibility of the Echo increased to the level of the Votrax.[3]

Thus, there appears to be a difference in intelligibility between synthesizers, but strategies for using the machine can improve intelligibility once the user learns them; for example, the user can produce a word or phrase group at a time rather than a whole sentence when the message is at all lengthy. If a synthesizer is not intelligible, the inexperience of the user manipulating its variables may be at fault rather than the synthesizer itself.

● **Can the User Manipulate Variables of the Synthesizer to Increase Intelligibility?**

If there are strategies for improving intelligibility, then the ability of the user to manipulate these variables must be explored. An individual who has limited spelling ability may be able to spell well enough to write messages understood even by unfamiliar partners. To have words pronounced intelligibly by a synthesizer requires some modification in spelling or, depending on the particular aid, the use of a phonemic alphabet. The individual who is unable to modify spelling or learn to use a phonemic alphabet will have to depend on others to create words, resulting in greater dependency and a reliance on prestored phrases. In addition, the individual's ability to add pauses where needed and to manipulate pitch and inflection variables, all of which can greatly affect intelligibility, must be explored.

● **Can Partners Be Trained to Understand the Synthesizer?**

As one becomes more familiar with a synthesizer, one learns to understand it, just as it is possible to learn to understand the speech of many severely speech-impaired persons. Thus, there is a need for training both the user and partners to become habituated to the patterns of distortion produced by a particular synthesizer.

Partners may vary in their ability to become habituated, depending upon many factors. For example, developmentally delayed adults who are unable to spell and read may have greater difficulty learning to understand speech synthesis than those with greater literacy skills. This was the result of a study conducted by Morgan and Wolff[4] who investigated the relationship between speech ability and reading skills and the ability of developmentally delayed adults to comprehend the speech produced by synthesizers. The results revealed that reading ability had a significant effect on an individual's comprehension of synthesized speech, while speech ability had no significant effect. The implications of this study are that the reading ability of both speech-impaired individuals and their primary and potential communication partners should be taken into account prior to recommending aids with a speech synthesizer.

● Is Output Sufficiently Intelligible That a Visual Display Is Not Needed?

A decision as to whether messages will be intelligible enough without a display must be made before an aid is purchased. Visual displays often serve as back-ups for speech output; when speech cannot be understood the message also appears on the display, so that those partners who can read are able to read the message. However, if the individual will be communicating with those who cannot read or if the aid is planned to be used at a great distance from partners (e.g., over the phone), a display cannot be used as a supplement.

● Are There Times When Other Modes Would Be Better for Conversation?

This decision must be made based upon the user, the partners and the situations in which the aid will be used. For example, a familiar partner may prefer that the individual use a visual display for conversation because, by predicting messages as they are formulated, communication rate is increased. Another partner may have limited time for conversation and may prefer that the individual write messages or use a nonelectronic aid.

USING SPEECH SYNTHESIS TO SOUND OUT WORDS

The ability of a severely speech-impaired child to spell is crucial not only for pursuit of educational and vocational goals but also for effective communication. Without the ability to spell, a speech-impaired child must rely on others to supply the words they think he or she wants to say. Because so much of learning to spell is based upon sounding out, spelling has been a major problem for many speech-impaired children.

Of particular interest are recent attempts to use speech output to teach young speech-impaired children to spell. A speech output aid can be programmed to produce each of the phonemes of English, which would allow a child to sound out a word through the synthesizer even though unable to do so through speech. This gives the child a means for creating sounds phonetically at a very early age. By learning to sound out any word he or she hears, the child gains the ability to produce open-ended vocabularies without knowing how to spell.[5]

An attempt to use a speech output aid to teach a child to augment his speech by sounding out words is illustrated by Mark, a 9-year-old speech-impaired boy. Mark's speech could be understood by very familiar partners only when they knew the topic he was discussing. Strangers could not understand him at all. Mark began talking less and less as he began to realize how difficult it was for people to understand him. He also was resistant to using a communication board with words and phrases because it lacked so much of what he wanted to express and it was easier to let people figure out what he was trying to say. Those who worked with Mark wished that he could spell so at least he could give an initial letter cue to his partner when a word was not understood. In fact, Mark was in the process of learning to spell but was having difficulty doing so. It was thought that this was due to his inability to sound out words.

Thus, with the assistance of a speech synthesizer, a plan was developed to teach Mark to be able to select the initial sound of a word. A speech output aid was programmed to produce several initial consonant sounds and a vowel-consonant combination; e.g., *B, K, F,* and *A-T.* When his teacher gave him a word to spell, Mark could sound it out with the synthesizer. For example, she would say the word *bat* and Mark would press the square with the *B*, then the square with *A-T.* After Mark was able to do this, the teacher would eliminate the oral model and present him with a picture, whose name she asked him to produce through the synthesizer.

After several weeks, an improvement appeared in Mark's ability to give the first letter of a word presented to him by someone else. The next task would be to train him to give the first letter of a word he is trying to communicate but that is not understood by his partner.

USING SPEECH OUTPUT WITH VISUALLY-IMPAIRED INDIVIDUALS

Speech output provides speech/writing-impaired individuals who also have visual impairments with the ability to use a communication aid even though they are unable to see selection displays. This includes individuals with visual, perceptual, and discrimination deficits that may occur in cerebral palsy, brainstem CVAs, multiple sclerosis, traumatic brain injury, and other conditions.

In many cases, the visually impaired person may be able to use direct selection, e.g., selecting letters from a keyboard. A speech synthesizer can produce each item as it is selected, providing feedback as to whether the item selected is correct. The contents of the entire screen can also be spoken.

In other cases, the visually impaired individual is unable to use direct selection because of a physical disability. In order to use a communication aid, items can be presented through auditory scanning: each item is spoken aloud until the desired item is reached. The user then activates a switch to select the item.

In addition, the visually impaired individual can use speech output with Morse code. As the user produces the dots and dashes corresponding to letters of the alphabet, the aid speaks each letter, giving feedback as to the correctness of the selection.

REFERENCES

1. Vanderheiden, G. (1976). *Synthesized speech as a communication mode for non-vocal severely handicapped individuals*, (pp. 1–2). Madison, WI: Trace Center.
2. Vanderheiden, G. and Lloyd, L. (in press), in S.W. Blackstone (Ed.), *Augmentative Communication: An Introduction*, Rockville, MD: American Speech and Hearing Association.
3. Kraat, A. W. & Levinson, E. (1984). Intelligibility of two speech synthesizers used in augmentative communication devices for the severely speech impaired. Paper presented at the International Society for Augmentative and Alternative Communication Conference, Boston.
4. Morgan, M. L. & Wolff, G. J. (1984). Reading and verbal ability and single word comprehension of synthesized speech by developmentally delayed adults. Paper presented at the International Society for Augmentative and Alternative Communication, Boston.
5. Vanderheiden, G. (1984). Personal communication.

9

Visual Displays and Printers

TYPES OF VISUAL DISPLAYS AND PRINTERS

Visual displays or screens present characters: letters, punctuation, numbers, mathematical signs, and symbols. As the individual selects each item from the aid, it appears on the display. The degree varies as to how much the display allows the user to correct these entries. Usually the last letter selected can be omitted, but it is possible to have greater editing capabilities, depending on the aid being used. When the aid is turned off, whatever was on the display will disappear, which is why these displays are also called *soft copy*.

A visual display can be a full screen, a single line, or multiple lines (Fig. 9-1). A full screen, which can be stationary or portable, can display 80 characters across and 24 lines down, the amount of material on a double-spaced, typewritten page (Fig. 9-2). Single and multiple-line displays vary in the number of characters they can display at one time. For example, the multiple-line display that comes with the ZYGO Notebook, a highly portable aid, can display up to 40 characters across and 8 lines down (Fig. 9-3).

Depending on the length of the message, only part of it may be visible at any one time, resembling the moving display on billboard advertising. Some aids have a "memory buffer," which allows the individual to hold what has been written on the display in memory, up to a certain number of characters, while continuing to write. When needed, the stored items are recalled and displayed.[1]

The size of the characters on a visual display varies according to the overall size of the display and the number of characters that can be displayed on the screen at one time. Most characters are usually about $\frac{1}{4}-\frac{1}{2}$ inch high but can be larger (Fig. 9-4). In order to assist in seeing the characters, many displays are available with an adjustor, which allows the display to be angled for best viewing.

Printed material can be produced through a strip, wide-column, or full-page printer (Fig. 9-5). The printed material is permanent; i.e., it does not disappear after it is produced, which is why it is also called *hard copy*. Strip or wide-column printers vary in the width of paper produced. A strip is usually $\frac{1}{4}$ inch wide, while a wide column can vary. A full-page printer produces printed material on standard $8\frac{1}{2} \times 11$ inch paper.

FIGURE 9-1. Examples of full screen, single-line, and multi-line visual displays. (Photo by Corbit's Studio, Bridgeport, CT.)

FIGURE 9-2. The Equalizer, an electronic communication aid with a portable full-screen display. (Photo courtesy of Words +, Inc., Sunnyvale, CA.)

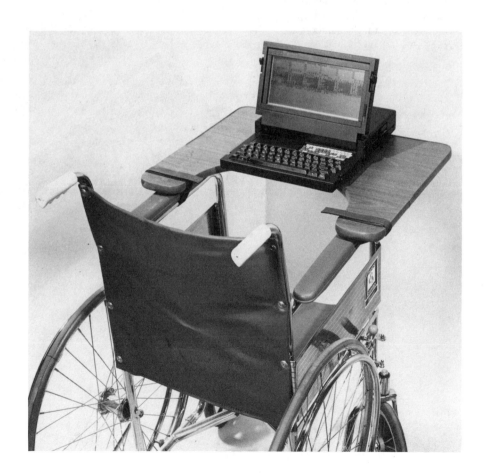

FIGURE 9-3. The ZYGO Notebook with a multi-line display. (Photo courtesy of ZYGO Industries, Portland, OR.)

FIGURE 9-4. The Talking 100, an electronic aid displaying large-size characters. (Photo courtesy of Commetrics, Ltd. St. Lambert, QUE.)

FIGURE 9-5. Examples of strip, wide column, and stationary printers available with electronic communication aids. (Photo by Corbit's Studio.)

While the strip or wide-column printer is usually manufactured as part of a portable aid, a portable wide column or full-page printer can be purchased separately. Some even can be snapped directly on the back of an aid (Fig. 9-6). Other full-page printers require electric current and can be used only for stationary applications.

Printers produce characters through heat or through ink. Over a period of time, the characters produced through heat can fade. They also fade if covered by scotch tape or other protective coating. The characters printed with ink are more durable.

FIGURE 9-6. The Hush Printer, a portable full-page printer that snaps onto the back of an electronic communication aid. (Photo courtesy of the Prentke Romich Company, Wooster, OH.)

EVALUATING VISUAL DISPLAYS AND PRINTERS

Visual displays provide an erasable, full-sentence presentation on an electronic display. As soon as the aid is turned off, the message disappears. Printers provide a permanent display, allowing written material to be printed and presented independent of the aid.

The capabilities provided by display permanence were discussed in Chapter 5. For conversation, a visual display usually is more effective because messages are easier to view than on a printer. A visual display provides the user access to other words through displaying cues and provides the partner with time to decipher messages, in addition to providing the partner continuous feedback.

The temporary nature of a display also may be more desirable than a printer for conversation. When individuals have all their conversation printed on paper for anyone to see, this can become quite embarrassing. One individual with a communication aid that printed on a narrow tape often would get into trouble when the wrong person read a scrap of paper. The individual referred to this as his "Nixon complex." He was always getting into trouble because of incriminating tapes that had been left behind.[2]

While a visual display may be more effective for conversation, a printer is essential for writing, in order to pursue academic and vocational goals, as well as for messaging.

Correctability is most effectively provided through a visible correctable display, as compared with printed or speech output, because the user easily can go back and modify the output before it is presented.[2]

When a visual display is used with a printer, the user can edit the output before it is printed permanently, which is important for writing. This enables the individual to produce work equal in quality to that of able-bodied persons. The greater the editing capabilities of the aid, the more extensively the individual can correct the work. Both displays and printers rate high intelligibility as long as the partner can read printed English. It is also easier for the partner to read an entire printed or displayed message than to piece it together, as is required with a nonelectronic aid.

The display enables the partner to study a message if there is any difficulty in deciphering it. For example, if an individual has spelling abilities that are functional for communication purposes, his or her messages may be understood when he or she prints them. When he or she tries to produce them through speech output, they may not be as intelligible due to the spelling modifications often required.

A visual display can supplement a message produced through speech output; i.e., a partner who does not understand the speech can look at the display. The display may also enable the user to produce more intelligible messages through speech output by allowing him or her to see the words as they are formulated and experiment with different spellings before they are presented by a speech synthesizer.

A visual display also is used to list the programming procedures used with some electronic aids; i.e., as one step of the procedure is performed, the next step to be performed is displayed.

Messages produced through printed or speech output are programmed at the same rate. However, a display can increase the rate of presentation of a message because the partner can read it on the visual display as it is being produced, allowing prediction of messages before they are completed. Of course, some individuals will not want the partner to predict, especially if the prediction is wrong. If a message produced on a visual display or printer is more intelligible to a partner than one produced through speech, there will be less need for repeating messages, and so the rate is increased.

A visual display rates high in assertability because the continuous feedback it provides assists in maintaining conversational control. A partner who must wait for the entire message to be produced before it is presented may lose attention or become involved in some other activity. The visual display takes the place, to some extent, of the normal feedback able-bodied persons give to each other during conversation to hold each other's attention.

Visual displays and printers greatly increase the independence of an individual, who can produce written material without a scribe constantly present. It also eliminates the possibility that the scribe is actually doing the work for the individual or embellishing upon it.

A display also provides independence in face-to-face conversation but not to as great a degree as speech output, because the partner must still pay close visual attention to the message. However, there is greater independence with a visual display than with a nonelectronic aid because there is no need for the partner to piece each item together.

The degree to which a visual display can project a message depends upon two features. One is the size of the characters. The larger the characters, the further away the partner can be from the display. The second is the position of the display. If the display faces only the aid user, conversation will be limited to those who can physically position themselves close enough to see the display. Some aids have two displays, one facing the user and the other facing the partner, which can be used to conduct conversations with partners at a distance, in a group, or in a more natural face-to-face position. In comparison to a visual display, a printer does not project well because the character size is small, requiring the partner to be in close physical proximity in order to read a message.

EXAMPLE: THE IMPORTANCE OF A VISUAL DISPLAY AND PRINTER

Janet, a severely speech-impaired woman, lived in a large, chronic-care, rehabilitation hospital. She communicated through yes/no responses, facial expression, a nonelectronic aid, and a portable electronic scanning aid with speech output, visual display, and printer.

Only a few hospital staff assigned to work with her actually had face-to-face conversations with Janet. When they did, they preferred to use her nonelectronic aid because communication was faster.

When Janet came into contact with many of the nurses, nurses' aids, physicians, and administrative staff members, she often had only her nonelectronic aid available. For example, if Janet were lying in bed ready for sleep, her electronic aid would not be set up; if she were being dressed, she could not control it. At those times, most of the staff would use the 20-question approach rather than the nonelectronic aid, because they found it to be faster. Others who worked with her did not know how to use the nonelectronic aid, because they had not been trained. When Janet had her electronic aid available, many of the staff members said they did not understand its speech output.

Because Janet had so little opportunity for direct conversation, she greatly relied on her visual display and printer to prepare messages in advance. To partners who did not have the time to talk with her or were not there on weekends and holidays, Janet would print messages about events that happened while the partners were away or requests for partners to do errands and chores. To the nurses, physicians, attendants, etc., the messages concerned questions about treatment, requests about dressing, feeding, handling, and other issues of personal care, complaints, thank you's, and all those things she would have liked to be able to say to these people. She also wrote messages to her family and friends and to other patients in the hospital.

Janet was not having a conversation with those she was writing to. The message receivers read the message and would usually respond directly to its contents. The partner would comment; then Janet would repond through yes/no, facial expressions, and whatever else she had available to her. When her electronic aid was again set up, she would write another message in response.

Although Janet had little chance to converse directly with these persons, she was able to communicate with them independently. There was always a look of amazement on the face of a new message receiver, as if it were unbelievable that Janet were capable of such an act. Some receivers learned how to use Janet's nonelectronic aid once they had realized that she was capable of communicating with them. Thus, as it does for many speech-impaired individuals, the visual display and printer both played very important roles for Janet.

EXAMPLE: USING A VISUAL DISPLAY, A PRINTER, AND SPEECH OUTPUT FOR COMMUNICATION

In selecting a communication aid for an individual, there is usually no one best method. Some users will need a nonelectronic aid, speech, visual display, and a printer, while others will need only one or two forms of output.

Stacy, an 18-year-old girl with athetoid cerebral palsy, used multiple outputs for communication. She was unable to produce sufficient speech for conversation, had no use of her upper extremities, and spent most of her time in a manual wheelchair, which she was unable to move independently. Stacy had attended a mainstream program in high school, where she learned to spell and read. Her communication system consisted of a nonelectronic alphabet board, whose letters she indicated through group-item scanning. She used this system to communicate with her teachers and several able-bodied students. At home, she and her mother relied primarily on facial expression, eye gaze, and yes/no responses, because Stacy's mother could not spell or read.

Upon graduating from high school, Stacy planned to go to college. She was fortunate enough to have a benefactor, who raised the money to buy Stacy an electronic aid in order to attend classes. A portable aid producing synthesized speech and a single-line visual display and printer, which she controlled through row-column scanning, was selected.

Stacy came to an outpatient clinic for weekly training sessions to learn how to use her electronic aid. At the clinic, she initially used her nonelectronic aid to converse with the therapists who were familiar with her. As she became more proficient in using her aid and as more messages were programmed that were useful to her, the nonelectronic aid was used less and less. She gradualy began to communicate using both the visual display and speech output, but the therapists found that they looked at the display and ignored the speech. This was because they were so used to the continuous feedback and rapid message production of the nonelectronic aid that they preferred the display. Stacy also used the display with other people who were very familiar with her; e.g., her resource room teacher from high school, who still came to visit. With partners who had communicated with her for many years using her nonelectronic aid, Stacy would spell messages on the display using the same abbreviation strategies, which greatly increased her rate of communication with them.

In school, Stacy used speech output for greetings, initiating conversation, interruptions, and other social interactions. When she wanted to answer a question in class, she would gain the teacher's attention through speech output. With the assistance of her attendant, she would then use the visual display to answer questions because the message could be produced faster by her attendant reading it aloud as she produced it than through speech output.

At school and at home, Stacy used the correctable display and printer to perform written assignments and to prepare messages in advance for the instructors, her fellow students and her attendant. Stacy's mother, unable to read, preferred that she use speech output. Whole words and phrases that Stacy frequently used at home had been programmed into the aid, so that she could produce them rapidly. For the mother, speech output gave her the opportunity to communicate with Stacy by more than just yes/no questions and guesses.

Thus, the communication needs of this particular individual were best met by multiple outputs.

REFERENCES

1. Kraat, A. W. (1982). Output modes available in communication devices. Paper presented at Communication Aids Workshop, West Lake, OH.
2. Vanderheiden, G. (1986). Personal communication.

PART IV

Selection Techniques For Augmentative Communication Aids

COMPARING THE SELECTION TECHNIQUES OF NONELECTRONIC AND ELECTRONIC AIDS

Because many speech/writing-impaired individuals are also severely physically disabled, the technique they use to select items is of great importance. Selection must be accomplished accurately, so that the message is intelligible to the partner. It must also be accomplished rapidly in order for the individual to maintain conversational control.

There are three selection techniques: direct selection, scanning, or directed scanning (a combination of these two approaches). In addition, various encoding techniques can be used with either direct selection or scanning.

Selection techniques can be evaluated along several dimensions: independence, rate, accessibility, and flexibility (see Chapter 5 for a description of these dimensions).

In general, electronic selection techniques provide greater independence in producing messages than nonelectronic techniques. A partner is not required to point to items for the individual or to flip displays or charts, as is so often required with a nonelectronic aid.

However, electronic selection-based techniques require greater physical control, because the target areas of an electronic aid demand either direct activation or activation through a switch to select desired items. Depending on the design of the aid and the selection technique being used, this will require a certain range of motion, accuracy of movement, and degree of pressure. In comparison, selecting items from a nonelectronic aid only requires the user to indicate a target that displays an item (e.g., point to a letter on a letter board) rather than activate a target. As a result, the individual can be less accurate and make selections more rapidly.

The greater physical control required by electronic selection techniques affects the aid's accessibility because the individual may have to be specially positioned to achieve the needed control. An aid that requires the individual to be optimally positioned in a wheelchair or other seating unit for use is less accessible than an aid that can be used in various positions.

Another difference between the selection techniques of these two types of aids is their flexibility. A nonelectronic aid is custom-made to meet the abilities of a particular user, while an electronic aid usually is manufactured for a general group of physically disabled persons. This means that, to use an electronic aid, the individual must have the physical abilities required to select items.

In order to provide greater flexibility, many electronic aids offer more than one selection technique. The advantage of this is the greater range of options available to the user, who may still be able to use the same aid when physical skills improve or deteriorate. The user can also use one technique when optimally positioned and another in times of less physical control.

In addition, many electronic aids offer as much flexibility as possible within a specific technique. For example, if an aid is controlled through scanning, a variable rate of scanning allows adjusting the device to the user's abilities.

Thus, while electronic selection techniques provide the individual with greater independence in selecting items than nonelectronic aids, their selection techniques may be less rapid to use and be less accessible to the user. These differences can result in the use of one selection technique with a nonelectronic aid and another with an electronic aid.

10 Direct Selection and Scanning

Direct selection refers to techniques in which the speech/writing-impaired individual points directly to a desired item in some manner. Because it is rapid and simple, it is the most conducive approach to communication. Examples of the use of direct selection are pointing to the letters of the alphabet printed on a board, pointing to a desired object, or typing.[1] While pointing with a finger is most common, direct selection can also be accomplished using any body part that has sufficient physical control.

Many individuals who do not have sufficient upper extremity control to directly select items can use head movement. This can be accomplished through the use of an extension device, such as a headstick or a chinstick (Fig. 10-1). The use of a headstick, like any direct selection technique, requires adequate range of motion to indicate a large enough number of items to be functional for communication. Individuals with limited head movement may be able to directly select items through the use of a light beam worn on the head. Even with limited movement, an individual can direct the light to shine on target areas. A light beam requires less range of motion than a headstick but enables the individual to select items within a large area. An example of this type of device is the Viewpoint Optical Indicator manufactured by the Prentke Romich Company (Fig. 10-2).

A light beam can also be used as an alternative for individuals who lack adequate control to use a headstick, because it requires less effort. It is also less cosmetically interfering than a headstick, because it is smaller. Its limitation is that it cannot be used to manipulate or to activate objects or devices.

The light beam can be used by young severely physically disabled children as an initial selection technique, even if they do not have fine pointing accuracy or a wide range of motion. It can be used to request items by pointing, to attract the attention of others by shining a light at them, and to respond and participate in classroom activities. This

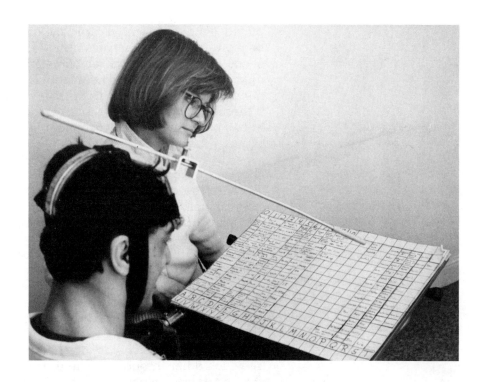

FIGURE 10-1. Use of a headstick to directly select items from a nonelectronic communication aid. (Photo by Corbit's Studio, Bridgeport, CT.)

FIGURE 10-2. Use of the Viewpoint Optical Indicator, a light beam worn on the forehead, to directly select items from a nonelectronic communication aid. (Photo by Corbit's Studio.)

provides the child with a rapid means of selecting items, which may be more motivating than scanning. The light beam can also be used in conjunction with other selection techniques; e.g., the child uses the light beam to participate in an activity where there are only a limited number of items to select from, as learning to recognize the numbers 0 through 10. For conversation, the child uses scanning because it allows indicating a greater number of items than can be selected with the light beam.

The individual's eyes can also be used to directly select items, but there are two disadvantages to using eyes with a nonelectronic aid. Because the eyes are used for looking, an eye gaze system may be confusing if that is not confused if the individual suddenly looks around during a signal or while controlling the aid. In addition, it is difficult for a partner to see exactly where the user is looking unless only a small number of widely spaced items is used.[2] With a technique that uses direct eye gaze, called Eye Link,[3] items are indicated by eye contact. The technique is based on the principle that it is easier for the partner to tell whether the user is looking at him than looking at items on a display.[2] The selections to be indicated are displayed on a transparent sheet of plastic or acetate in a rectangular matrix. The partner holds the sheet facing the user so that they can see each other through it. The user then fixes his or her eyes on the desired item. The partner, watching the user's eyes, moves the board until eye contact is made through an individual square, indicating the desired selection (Fig. 10-3).

The advantages of Eye Link are the ease with which both the user and partner can be instructed in its use and the rapid rate of communication that can be achieved. However, the speech-impaired individual must have adequate ability to control eye gaze and the cognitive ability to learn how to use the technique. It also may be tiring for the partner, who must hold the sheet and constantly move it. While not all speech/writing-impaired individuals and partners will be able to use this technique or will prefer it, the technique can be used in many situations, especially when the user has no other aided system available in a particular environment or position.

FIGURE 10-3. An individual and her partner using Eye Link. (Drawing by Ava Barber, NY, NY.)

Electronic aids have been developed that enable an individual to activate a desired target through ocular motion; i.e., by looking at it. Several different techniques are used. Some systems measure eye motion or position of the eyes in the head, while others directly measure the direction or location of gaze in order to determine the target.[4] Ocular motion aids offer the use of direct selection to many speech/writing-impaired individuals who could not previously use this technique.

Correct positioning and seating, which greatly affect physical control, are crucial to an individual's ability to use direct selection. Very often, through trial and error, an individual who initially appears unable to use direct selection eventually is able to use this technique, when placed in an optimal position.[1] In addition, correct seating can greatly increase the rate of direct selection.

DEVELOPING DIRECT SELECTION

An individual who is initially unable to use direct selection may gradually develop this ability when seated properly. This often happens with young children who have limited upper extremity or head control and who have not used these body parts in any purposeful manner. When given the opportunity to use these body parts to indicate what they want and the chance to practice these skills consistently, many children eventually develop functional direct selection abilities.

For example, Jennifer, an 8-year-old speech-impaired child with severe atheotid movements of the upper extremities, appeared unable to use her arms and hands for any but very gross activities. She communicated through vocalizations, responding to yes/no questions through head movements, eye pointing, and facial expression.

Initially, she was given a light beam to directly select objects, to gain attention, and to participate in activities in the classroom and at home. Because her pointing with the light beam was not very accurate, she was also given a nonelectronic aid, consisting of an encoded display whose items she indicated through eye gaze. In addition, three messages written on large cards that she frequently used were placed on her lapboard, spaced far enough apart so that she could indicate them with her eyes and her partner could tell where she was looking. These were placed on the lapboard so they would be accessible to her even if her eye gaze board were not available. The messages were (1) I want to go to the bathroom, (2) I want to go on the floor, and (3) Take the light beam off. All three were very important to her, and she had previously been unable to clearly communicate these messages through unaided techniques.

Soon after the messages were placed on her board, Jennifer began to accurately point to the one on the right with her right hand, to the one on the left with her left hand, and to the one in the middle with either hand. Other messages then were added gradually to the lapboard. Although Jennifer was able to use both hands to point, she was more accurate with the right than with the left, so messages on the right were placed in smaller target areas, allowing more of them to be displayed, while messages on the left were larger (Fig. 10-4). Use of the eye gaze system gradually was faded out.

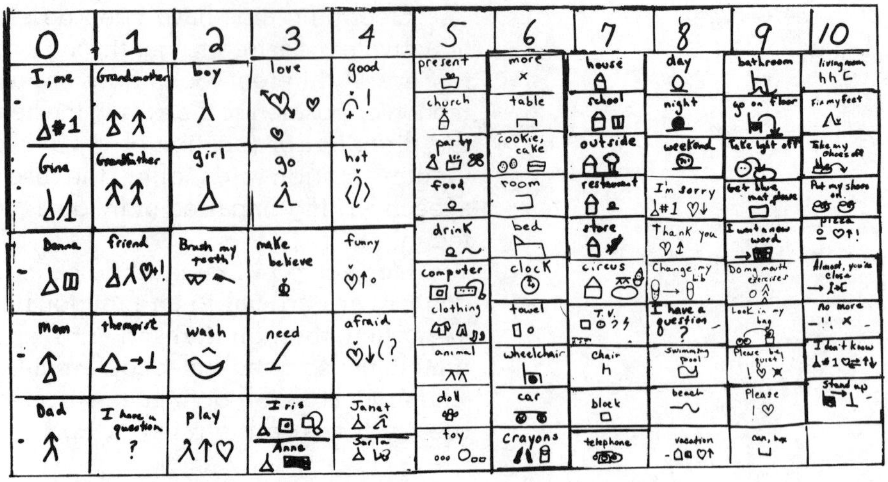

FIGURE 10-4. Board with items placed in larger target areas on the left and smaller areas on the right to accommodate the user's accuracy of pointing. (Photo by Corbit's Studio. The Blissymbols appearing in the photograph have been hand-drawn and are not to be considered for useage beyond this customized display. For standard Blissymbols, see Blissymbols For Use [Hehner, 1980].)

When Jennifer's pointing was not entirely accurate (she sometimes pointed to several adjacent target areas at once), she was encouraged to be more accurate (but not pressured to do so). If her message was unclear, her partner would use a point and scan technique to name each item Jennifer had pointed to until she indicated the one she wanted. Often, the partner could guess what the message was by knowing the topic of the conversation. Eventually, point and scan was rarely used, because Jennifer's pointing became more accurate. She soon was able to use a board displaying 150 items (Fig. 10-5).

This occurrence is not uncommon with children. Initially, they can be given the least effortful and most accurate means of indicating items, usually through scanning or eye gaze. In addition, they can be given the opportunity to use direct selection. In this way, the child is able to practice direct selection for a functional and motivating purpose, while not being pressured to do so because other means of selection are available.

ACTIVATING TARGETS OF ELECTRONIC DIRECT SELECTION AIDS

The selection display of an electronic aid consists of target areas the individual must be able to accurately activate rather than merely indicate. If inaccurate, an undesired message may be produced by the aid. Thus, direct selection with an electronic aid requires greater physical ability than with a nonelectronic aid.

The type of target on an electronic aid will determine the physical abilities needed to activate it. Basically, targets can be categorized according to whether they require pressure for activation.

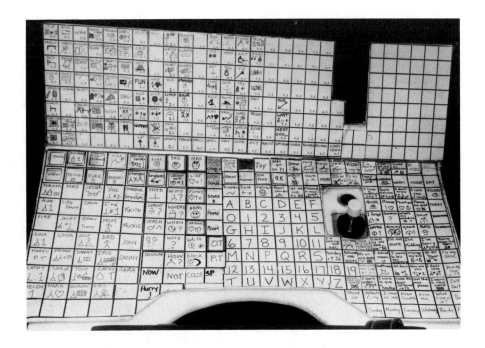

FIGURE 10-5. Board with an increased number of items and a smaller target size. (Photo by Corbit's Studio. The Blissymbols appearing in the photograph have been hand-drawn and are not to be considered for useage beyond this customized display. For standard Blissymbols, see Blissymbols For Use [Hehner, 1980].)

Targets Requiring Pressure to Be Activated

These targets can consist of a key, button, or pressure-sensitive membrane surface (Fig. 10-6). The target can be activated through pressure exerted directly by a body part (hand, finger, foot, arm, or leg) or with a headpointer, mouthstick, a handheld device, or any other device that can be used to exert pressure.

Depending on the sensitivity of the target, too much pressure can result in an item being activated several times, while too little pressure can result in a target not being activated at all. Uncontrolled movements can activate unwanted targets, as the individual moves from one selection to the next. Many aids with targets requiring pressure have guards to help prevent random activation.

A guard is a firm plate that fits over the aid's selection display with holes located over each target area (Fig. 10-7). The guard can perform several functions. It can prevent accidental depression of undesired areas. It can provide needed guidance for the finger or other body part or extension device (such as a headpointer) that is activating the desired target. Depending upon the construction of the guard, it can support the individual's hand and provide a surface for the user to push against for steady movements.[5] The use of a guard can make it possible for an individual to use an electronic aid that otherwise might require too much fine accuracy of movement.

Targets Requiring No Pressure in Order to Be Activated

This type of target contains an array of LEDs (light emitted diodes) on a selection display that can be detected with a photodetector, usually mounted in some type of extension device and worn on the head. A sequencing routine turns on and off each LED individually and in a prearranged pattern. Because the sequencing is very fast, the LED appears to be dimly lit. The photodetector detects the first LED that is lit in its field of view. The LED that is detected then lights up brightly, indicating the target being pointed to. A particular item is activated

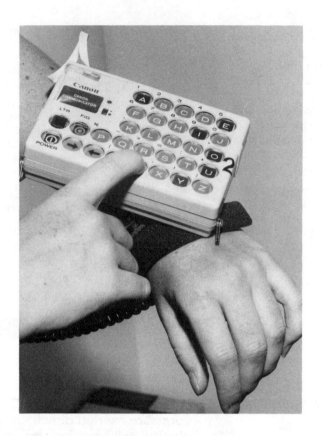

FIGURE 10-6. The Canon Communicator, an electronic aid which is activated by exerting pressure on its keys. (Photo by Corbit's Studio.)

FIGURE 10-7. A keyguard used with the Apple IIe computer to prevent random activation of the keys. (Photo by Corbit's Studio.)

by pointing at it for a predefined period of time. The individual moves his or her head to change the area that is detected and allow activation of different targets. The time period required before a target is activated can be adjusted according to the abilities of the user, to prevent unwanted selections as he or she moves from one target to the next.[6]

The Light Talker is an electronic aid that can be controlled in this manner. The target areas of this aid are activated by the Optical Headpointer, which the individual wears (Fig. 10-8).

COMPARING NONELECTRONIC AND ELECTRONIC DIRECT SELECTION

Both nonelectronic and electronic aids require that the individual have a certain range of motion and a certain accuracy of pointing with the body part that is directly selecting items. Range of motion determines how far the individual can move within a given area, while accuracy determines how small a target area can be pointed to within that area. The greater these abilities, the more target areas the individual can have in which to display or store vocabulary items.

Because an electronic aid's selection display is relatively fixed in design, the individual must have the ability to activate its targets, in contrast to the display area of a nonelectronic aid, which can be arranged to accommodate the individual's physical abilities. For example, if an electronic aid has 128 targets, each measuring 1 × 2 inches, then the individual must have the range of motion and accuracy of movement to reach these targets.

In certain aids, the size and location of target areas can be changed to some extent to accommodate those who cannot handle very small targets or who have better range of motion at one location of the aid than another. However, the type of target usually cannot be changed once it is manufactured.

FIGURE 10-8. The Optical Headpointer used to control Light Talker. (Photo by Corbit's Studio).

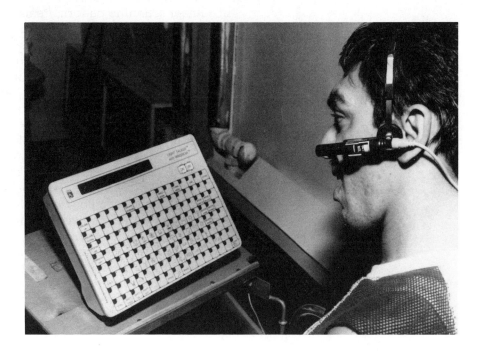

Thus, in order to control an electronic direct selection aid, the individual needs a greater degree of physical ability than to select items from a nonelectronic aid. The number, size, location, and type of targets will determine the physical abilities the speech/writing-impaired individual needs to control it.

Because of the abilities required to use an electronic direct selection aid, finding an aid that the user can control adequately may be difficult. In many cases, a speech/writing-impaired individual who uses direct selection to select items with a nonelectronic aid may be unable to use this technique with an electronic aid. In other cases, although the individual can use a direct selection technique when properly positioned, he may be unable to do so when lying in bed, on a mat receiving physical therapy, being dressed, etc. In these cases, a scanning technique can be used.

SCANNING PATTERNS

Scanning involves presenting items until the individual indicates that the desired item has been reached. A familiar example of scanning is Twenty Questions, where a series of questions, answered by yes or no, are presented to the individual, one at a time, until the question asker finds out the desired information. This technique is often used to communicate with severely speech-impaired individuals when other techniques are not available or not sufficiently effective to express a message.

Scanning often is thought of as the last-resort selection technique because it is slower than direct selection. However, depending on the physical abilities of a particular user, scanning can be more rapid and effective than other methods. Additionally, many speech/writing-impaired individuals who can use direct selection in one situation will need to use scanning in others.

In a linear scanning pattern, items are scanned one at a time until the individual indicates the desired item. This is illustrated in Figure 10-9. A speech-impaired individual is using linear scanning to spell a word. She indicates unwanted items to her partner by not responding and the desired letter by responding with a smile. In Step 1, the partner points to the letter *A*. The individual does not respond, indicating, "No, that's not the letter I want." In Step 2, the partner points to the letter *B* and again the individual does not respond. In Step 3, the partner points to the letter *C*. The individual smiles, indicating "Yes, that is the letter I want."

In order to decrease the time it takes to make a selection, group-item scanning can be used. The most commonly used group-item pattern is row-column scanning, where items are arranged in rows. Each row is presented to the individual who must indicate when the row containing the desired item he or she wants is reached. Each item in the row is then presented one at a time until the individual again indicates when the desired item is reached. Row-column scanning increases communication rate by decreasing the number of items that must be presented to the user before he or she makes a selection.[2]

Step 1

Step 2

Step 3

FIGURE 10-9. An example of linear scanning with a non-electronic communication aid. (Drawing by Ava Barber.)

This is illustrated in Figure 10-10, where the individual is using row-column scanning to spell a word. In Step 1, the partner points to the first row and the individual indicates by not responding, "No, the letter I want is not in that row." In Step 2, the partner points to the second row and, again, the individual indicates "No." In Step 3, the partner points to third row and the individual indicates "Yes" with a smile, meaning that the letter she wants is in that row. The partner then begins to scan each letter in the row. When she reaches the second letter (Step 4), the individual indicates "Yes," meaning that she wants to select the letter *N*.

FIGURE 10-10. An example of row-column scanning with a non-electronic communication aid. (Drawing by Ava Barber.)

Step 1

Step 2

Step 3

Step 4

An electronic scanning aid presents items to the user in a continuous, uniform pattern. The individual selects a desired item through the use of a single switch, which acts as an interface between user and aid.

An example of this pattern is used by the scanning aids manufactured by ZYGO Industries, Inc., illustrated in Figure 10-11. The selection display of the aids consist of eight rows of targets, with eight targets in each row. Each target contains an LED. When turned on, the aid automatically begins row scanning where each full row of eight LED targets illuminates and steps vertically, row to row, in continuous succession, from the top to the bottom (Step 1). This starts over again until the first switch actuation by the user converts the pattern to column scanning (Step 2), then a single light scans horizontally (again in continuous succession), from left to right within the selected row, until the user's second switch actuation stops the scan at the desired target. A flashing of the selected LED visually confirms the actual selection which either is displayed on a visual display, printed, or spoken.[7]

Most electronic aids allow the scan rate to be adjusted for a particular user, but the scan rate is usually linear; i.e., it is uniform throughout the scan pattern. After the individual selects an item, row scanning immediately begins at the same rate. If an individual wants to select an item in the first three rows or the first three columns of the selection display, it easily can be missed the first time around and the vertical scanning pattern must then go through a complete cycle before the selection can be made, decreasing the communication rate. In order to alleviate this, ZYGO developed a nonlinear scan presentation. Following switch actuation, scanning does not begin again at the same rate. Rather, it immediately slows down and incrementally increases speed row to row or column to column up to the set linear rate.[7]

FIGURE 10-11. An example of row-column scanning as used in ZYGO electronic communication aids. (Drawing courtesy of ZYGO Industries, Inc., Portland, OR.)

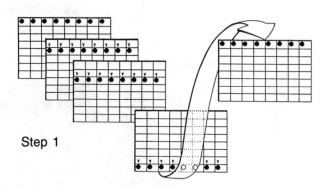

Step 1

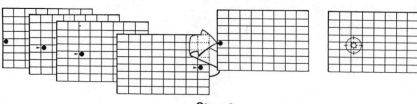

Step 2

With nonelectronic scanning, in contrast, the partner can adjust the pattern according to the user's abilities by increasing or decreasing the scan rate, skipping rows and columns, scanning backwards and forwards, etc. Thus, because nonelectronic scanning is more flexible, it can be faster, although the user must depend on a partner to present items for selection.

As with direct selection, greater physical ability is required to use an electronic scanning technique than a nonelectronic one. This is because the user must have a body part (called a control site) capable of activating a switch rather than merely indicating, "Yes, that is the item I want." Greater cognitive abilities may also be required because the user must select the items independently from the aid's display without assistance from the partner.

EXAMPLE: HOW NONELECTRONIC SCANNING CAN BE MORE EFFECTIVE THAN ELECTRONIC SCANNING

Amelia, a 47-year-old woman, became quadriplegic and severely speech-impaired due to a brainstem CVA incurred at the age of 35. One night, as Amelia was in her bed at the chronic care hospital where she lived, she witnessed an attendant abusing another patient. The next day, she printed out what she had seen on her electronic communication aid, which she controlled through scanning, and delivered it to her speech pathologist. The event was reported, and eventually the hospital fired the attendant. However, the attendant's union appealed the firing and a hearing was held between the hospital and the union to determine if the attendant had been justly dismissed. Amelia was called upon to testify as to what she had witnessed.

Much to everyone's surprise, Amelia gave her testimony, not through the use of her scanning electronic aid, but through a simple letter/phrase board made of paper and ink, which she used for conversation with familiar partners. The letters on the board were arranged by frequency of occurrence. Additionally, phrases frequently used during testimony were added, such as "I don't remember." Amelia was able to use this board very quickly with her speech pathologist, who acted as translator during the hearing. They also arranged between them that by rotating her fist, Amelia could indicate that she wanted to spell out a reply rather than to merely answer yes or no to the attorney's questions. By closing her eyes, she indicated that she did not understand a particular question.

Although Amelia was dependent on her speech pathologist to act as translator, she chose the nonelectronic aid over the electronic one because it was faster. If the electronic aid had been used, the testimony would have taken much longer, Amelia would have fatigued more rapidly, the judge would have become impatient, and the testimony would probably not have been anywhere as effective as it was. Ultimately, because of Amelia's testimony, the attendant was not reinstated.

Therefore, in Amelia's case and that of many others, the nonelectronic aid was more effective in a particular situation than an electronic aid would have been, because it provided a more rapid, effective means of face-to-face conversation.[8]

ADVANTAGES AND DISADVANTAGES OF SCANNING

The major advantage of scanning is that it can be used by a severely physically disabled individual who cannot directly select items. Because scanning requires only minimal movement, its use is less dependent on good positioning, although positioning is still important. This means that an individual who is not optimally positioned can still indicate items or control the aid when in bed, on the floor, on a mat, or prior to the point when the individual has been positioned well enough to use direct selection. Scanning rate can also be modified to accommodate the individual's response time, either with a nonelectronic aid by the partner (the partner can indicate items faster or slower as required) or with an electronic aid through a control setting. In addition, because scanning requires less physical ability, it is less physically fatiguing over a period of time and, so, may be a better selection for an individual who tires easily.

Another advantage of scanning is that it can be used by visually impaired individuals who cannot see vocabulary items on a display, although they might have the physical ability to point to them. This can be done through the use of auditory rather than visual presentation of items to the individual. Using an unaided scanning technique, the partner presents items to the individual aloud rather than pointing to them on a display. With an electronic aid, items are presented through the use of speech output. This can be done in a linear pattern, where each item is spoken until the desired one is reached. It can also be done in a group-item manner if the individual has memorized which items are in each group. For example, the name of each group is spoken (group 1, group 2) until the individual indicates when the group that contains the desired item is reached. The name of each item within the group is then spoken until the individual again indicates when the desired item has been reached.

There are several disadvantages to scanning. The technique can be very slow because of the amount of time spent pointing to unwanted items before the desired one is reached. Because the individual is very passive, the technique may be less motivating. With a nonelectronic technique, the partner must be physically capable of scanning items for the individual, pointing to each item or saying each item out loud. Both nonelectronic and electronic scanning require a great deal of cooperation and time from partners. Since speed is such an important factor in conversation, scanning with any aid may limit the amount of interaction between the partner and the speech-impaired individual.

Additionally, although it requires less physical control, the use of scanning requires greater cognitive abilities than direct selection. The individual must be able to attend to the targets on the aid's display while waiting to indicate the desired item. It also requires focusing attention on several things at once: locating the desired item, rejecting unwanted items, focusing on the partner or the cursor to indicate the desired item before it is passed over. Unless an electronic aid producing the message on a visual display is used, the user must have greater memory ability because he or she must remember each item that has been indicated. This can be difficult if the message is of any length, unless the partner writes down each item as the individual indicates it.[1]

DIRECTED SCANNING

Directed scanning combines both direct selection and scanning by allowing the user to control the direction and timing of movement of a cursor or indicator to select an item. With electronic directed scanning, a single indicator is moved anywhere on the display panel with two to four switches. These switches represent the four directions ← LEFT UP ↑ DOWN ↓ RIGHT →. Only two switches are actually needed to select any target area on the panel (→ RIGHT ↓ DOWN), although four switches would greatly increase selection speed.

Directed scanning can be manipulated in two ways (Fig. 10-12). In a single-step scan, a single, momentary switch actuation moves the indicator one message area. In a multiple-step scan, maintaining any switch closure causes the indicator to scan in the selected direction until released. The speed of scan correlates directly to the scan rate control setting.[7]

Because directed scanning must be controlled through one switch that can provide multiple signals or through multiple switches, greater physical ability is required than to control a single switch. Whether this technique is faster than row-column scanning depends on the abilities of the particular individual using the technique.

FIGURE 10-12. An example of directed scanning as used in ZYGO electronic communication aids. (Drawing courtesy of ZYGO Industries, Inc.)

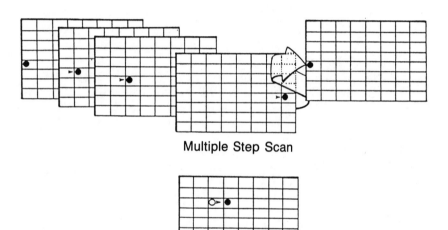

Multiple Step Scan

Single Step Scan

REFERENCES

1. Harris, D., & Vanderheiden, G. (1980). Enhancing the development of communicative interaction. In R. L. Schiefelbusch (Ed.), *Nonspeech language and communication: Analysis and intervention.* Baltimore: University Park Press.
2. Vanderheiden, G., & Lloyd, L. (in press). Communication systems and their components. In S. W. Blackstone (Ed.), *Augmentative communication: An introduction.* Rockville, MD: American Speech and Hearing Association.
3. Drinker, P. A., & Krupoff, S. (1981). Eye-link for non-vocal communication: Direct selection by eye contact. Paper presented at the Fourth Annual Conference on Rehabilitation Engineering, Washington, D.C.
4. Demasco, P., & Foulds, R. (1984). Overview of ocular communication systems. Paper presented at the International Society for Augmentative and Alternative Communication Conference, Boston.
5. Vanderheiden, P. J. (1985). Writing aids. In J. G. Webster et al. (Eds.), *Electronic devices for rehabilitation* (pp. 271–272). New York: John Wiley and Sons.
6. Gunderson, J. R. (1985). Interfacing the motor impaired. In J. G. Webster et al. (Eds.) *Electronic devices for rehabilitation* (pp. 209–211). New York: John Wiley and Sons.
7. ZYGO Industries, Inc. (1983). Computer products brochure. Portland, OR.
8. Fishman, I. (1983). Testimony of a nonspeaking witness. *Communication Outlook, 5, 23.*

11

Practical Considerations in Choosing and Using a Selection Technique

In choosing a selection technique for use with a communication aid, the speech pathologist must work closely with an occupational or physical therapist. These professionals have the knowledge of positioning and upper extremity control necessary to select the transmission technique that is best for the individual. However, members of each profession have different concerns. Occupational and physical therapists are concerned with the rehabilitation or development of physical abilities, while the speech pathologist is concerned with providing a functional means of communicating. These concerns often may conflict with each other.

It is crucial that conflicts be resolved through negotiation so that the individual receives the services needed from each discipline. Conflict frequently arises in two areas concerning selection techniques: positioning of the individual and arrangement of target areas.

Positioning

Correct seating and positioning are crucial to a physically disabled person's ability to achieve maximum physical functioning. Poor positioning makes everything more effortful for the individual, including communication. Thus, the disabled person must be properly positioned in all locations in which the aid most frequently will be used, including in a wheelchair, in bed, on the floor, or seated at a table.

The Conflict: An individual has the ability to directly select items with an electronic aid when properly positioned in a wheelchair. However, the physical or occupational therapist responsible for such positioning does not want to provide lateral supports, lapboards, or other types of adaptive equipment that can maintain the correct position in order to encourage the individual to develop the ability to keep erect on her own. While the individual is able to keep her body erect independently without positioning if reminded to do so, she is unable to use direct selection because all of her energy must be devoted to sitting up. This results in the individual having to use a scanning technique with her communication aid. In addition, she is unable to control the aid through scanning as quickly and accurately as she could if positioned correctly.

The Negotiation: In order to provide good positioning and still provide the individual with the experience of using her own muscles to position herself, the therapists arrange a separate time where the individual only works on self-positioning without any special equipment. In order to communicate during this time, a nonelectronic aid is designed with items she can indicate through scanning. At all other times, the individual is positioned with the support she needs to sit independently and control her electronic communication aid through direct selection.

Arrangement of Target Areas to Be Selected on an Aid's Display

The arrangement of target areas containing vocabulary items on an aid's selection display must be placed so they can be selected easily within the range of the individual's physical abilities. If using direct selection, target areas must be placed within the individual's range of motion and must be large enough to indicate accurately, whether pointing with a finger, a headstick, etc. If scanning is used, target areas must be placed so that the individual can follow a partner's movements with his or her eyes as the partner scans each item. Target placement must not require movement beyond the individual's range of motion or in a direction that presents difficulty.

The Conflict: An individual can directly select items with his left hand while the range of motion of his right arm is limited. The occupational/physical therapist wants to place target areas so that he must use the right hand to select items, rather than the better hand, to encourage the individual to use the right arm more to improve its functioning. As a result, the individual cannot select a sufficient number of items to be functional for conversation.

The Negotiation: A specific time is designated when the individual receives treatment from the occupational/physical therapist for the right arm or performs activities with that arm. During that time period, he can still use his left hand with his communication aid while he receives treatment to improve use of the right arm. If the occupational/physical therapist does not want him to use the left arm during treatments, the individual can indicate items on his aid through scanning.

Although many conflicts can arise, the principle of negotiation remains the same. Rather than interfering with the individual's ability to functionally communicate or interfering with the development or rehabilitation of physical abilities, negotiating with other professionals will result in the individual receiving all the services required.

EXAMPLE: THE DIFFICULTY OF SELECTING AN ELECTRONIC TECHNIQUE

It is often difficult for an individual who uses a nonelectronic selection technique to shift to an electronic technique. For one reason, whatever control site is being used to indicate a selection may not be capable of activating a target or controlling a switch with an electronic aid. As a result, the individual may have to use a slower technique or a different control site.

Another reason is that the electronic aid may not be accessible to the individual for all activities and in all environments in which the nonelectronic aid can be used. This is because controlling the aid may require optimal positioning and proper mounting of the aid, and control switch if also used. As a result, when out of the wheelchair or other seating unit or in activities where not optimally positioned, the individual will not be able to use the electronic aid.

This can result in the speech/writing-impaired individual using one selection technique with a nonelectronic aid and another, slower technique with an electronic aid. For example, Jennifer, an 8-year-old severely speech-impaired child with athetoid cerebral palsy, uses a nonelectronic aid consisting of approximately 200 words, phrases, and Blissymbols placed on the laptray of her wheelchair. The aid has been custom-made to accommodate her particular abilities so that she is able to indicate items through direct selection. On the right side of the aid, target areas are 1 × 1 inch, because she can accurately point to an area this size; while on the left side, targets are 1 × 2 inches because her pointing is not as accurate with her left hand.

Jennifer needs an electronic aid for several reasons. She needs to be able to converse with other students in her class, participate in classroom and group activities, and speak over the phone. She also needs to be able to do her schoolwork independently and prepare materials in advance. Finally, as there is no more room to place items on the display of her nonelectronic aid, an electronic aid with programming capability would give her access to a larger vocabulary.

Jennifer was evaluated with a portable direct selection aid producing printed and speech output for a period of one month. It was assumed that because she used direct selection with her nonelectronic aid, she would be able to do so with an electronic aid as well. Prior to this period of trial use, her seating was optimized with lateral supports and other adaptive equipment on her wheelchair to maximize her physical control. A custom-made mounting system was designed to hold the aid on the lapboard.

Despite all of this, Jennifer still had great difficulty controlling the aid. She would activate unwanted targets as she moved from one to the next or exerted too much pressure on a target.

For the present, the only alternative for Jennifer appears to be an electronic aid controlled through scanning. Although she can use scanning for writing needs, it will not be as effective for conversation because familiar partners can converse with Jennifer, using her nonelectronic aid, much faster and more effectively. Although the electronic aid will make her more independent, the nonelectronic aid will probably still be used for face-to-face conversation. Therefore, a selection decision will be postponed while her therapists search for a direct selection aid that Jennifer can control or while they find another way of modifying her seating to improve her physical control.

USING NONELECTRONIC SCANNING AS A BACK-UP TO AN ELECTRONIC AID

In situations where the ability to control an electronic aid is affected, an individual should have a nonelectronic aid as a back-up. Because nonelectronic scanning usually is less dependent on positioning and requires minimal physical movement, compared with direct selection, and is more obvious to an untrained partner than an encoding technique, it is often used in these situations.

One situation that can result in the need for a nonelectronic back-up is any change in the individual's positioning. Many individuals cannot use their electronic aids unless they are optimally positioned; e.g., only when in a wheelchair that has cushioning for trunk support, a laptray for upper extremity stability, footrests, and numerous other adaptations. This limites the accessibility of the aid to those situations when the individual is optimally positioned.

Thus, when not optimally positioned, the individual may be totally unable to control the electronic aid; e.g., when lying in bed, getting bathed and dressed, sitting in a dentist's chair, receiving physical therapy on a mat, etc. If this is the case, a nonelectronic aid must be available with a selection technique that can be used despite a change of positioning.

Amelia, who was previously described in the chapter on scanning, used her nonelectronic scanning alphabet board in many situations in which she would have been physically unable to control her electronic scanning aid. When she was being washed, dressed, fed, positioned, having her teeth cleaned, or her eyes examined, she did not have access to the control switch, which was mounted on her wheelchair. She could use her scanning alphabet board, however, in any position because all it required was indicating a desired item by looking up.

This situation occurs frequently with speech-impaired children, who are out of their chairs and on the floor, in the prone stander, and in various other positions throughout the day. A child who cannot control an electronic aid in these positions must have a nonelectronic aid to use.

Another situation that would call for a nonelectronic back-up is a temporary change in an individual's physical status that would affect the ability to control the electronic aid. Speech-impaired persons become ill, just like able-bodied persons, and some become ill even more frequently; for instance, aspiration pneumonia recurs among those with feeding or swallowing difficulties, which are common in this group. Speech-impaired individuals also are likely to undergo surgery more often; e.g., cerebral palsied children may undergo operations for hip dislocation and other orthopedic problems. Although these situations may be temporary, the individual still needs a nonelectronic aid, whose items easily can be selected, during this interim period.

12 Encoding Techniques

Encoding is a secondary technique that can be used with either direct selection or scanning. Use of a code allows the individual to indicate a small number of items (the code) that corresponds to a much larger vocabulary.[1]

When used with direct selection, encoding can increase the number of items available for communication beyond what the individual is capable of pointing to. For example, an individual has only sufficient range of motion and accuracy of pointing using a headpointer to point to six target areas, each measuring 2×4 inches, on a display measuring 12×4 inches. Although this amount is not sufficient to be functional for communication, it is sufficient for a code consisting of six elements. For example, 6 numbers, (1 through 6, each number placed in a target) can be used as elements of a code corresponding to letters of the alphabet.

Each letter is then assigned a code consisting of two numbers; e.g., 1–2 stands for the letter A. In order to spell a word, the individual points to the numbers corresponding to each letter. The code can be memorized by the individual and partners or a chart with the letters and their corresponding number codes can be placed so that the individual or partner can easily refer to it (Fig. 12-1).

Encoding is often used with nonelectronic eye gaze systems because of the limited amount of items that can be directly indicated with the eyes (see Chapter 10 on direct selection with the eyes for further discussion). Instead of directly indicating items, the individual indicates a code that is displayed on an eye gaze chart with code elements arranged so that the partner can tell which element the individual is looking at. The partner can then refer to a separate display which lists the code and the item it corresponds to.

Figure 12-2 illustrates the use of one type of eye gaze chart. The chart usually is made of clear plastic and is placed between the user and partner; e.g., mounted to a laptray. The partner sits or stands opposite the user. An open space is provided in the middle of the chart so that the partner can clearly follow the user's eye movements. This space also provides an area for the user to indicate a break between each code element by making eye contact with the partner.

FIGURE 12-1. An example of an encoding system used to increase the number of items available for communication beyond what the individual is capable of pointing to. (Drawing by Ava Barber, New York, NY.)

FIGURE 12-2. Use of an ETRAN-Number chart to indicate code elements with the eyes. (Drawing by Ava Barber.)

In this example, an ETRAN-Number chart is being used, where a two number code has been assigned to each item. In this example, the items are letters of the alphabet. However, letters, shapes, colors, or any other code elements that the individual can recognize can also be used.

If necessary, a chart displaying the code and the items it corresponds to can be placed where the user can refer to it, if it has not been memorized already. A chart must also be available for the partner's reference, but it can be hung below the ETRAN-Number chart or in a separate location.

In order to spell a word using the ETRAN-N chart, the user must select the two number code corresponding to the letters in it. Step 1 shows the user looking at the first number (6). She then must look back at the partner to indicate that is the first code element. In Step 2, she looks at the second number (3), then again looks back at the partner. The partner usually repeats each code element as the user indicates it, to ensure that it is correct, and then says the code (in this case, 6-3). In Step 3, the partner refers to a chart listing the codes and their corresponding items. The chart shows that 6-3 stands for the letter J.[2]

In addition to direct selection, encoding is used with scanning to decrease the time it takes for an individual to make selections. In the earlier example of the code consisting of two numbers from 1 through 6, it would take less time for an individual to select this code through scanning than to scan a display containing the entire alphabet.

Encoding can also be used to provide more message elements for the individual who needs a great number of items than can be visible on a selection display. For example, the size of the space available for the aid may limit the size of a selection display to 50 items. In order to expand the number of available items beyond this, a code can be used that corresponds to a separate display containing additional items, which is attached to the aid in some manner.

This use of a code is illustrated in Figure 12-3. The 9-year-old child using this aid can directly select all the items (totalling over 150 words and phrases in addition to the alphabet and numbers), placed on the part of the selection display on her laptray. However, the child is just learning to spell and is still dependent on the words and phrases made available to her by others, so that 150 items still is not sufficient to be functional for conversation.

Thus, attached to the aid is a separate display, with additional items the child is unable to directly select because they are beyond her range of motion. In order to indicate these, each item has been assigned a letter/number code that the child can indicate by directly selecting the numbers and letters on her display. For example, M-6 stands for the word *wash*.

Electronic aids use encoding in a manner similar to the previous example. Rather than having the items visible on a display, however, they are stored in the aid's memory. This provides the individual with a greater number of items because it usually is possible to store more than can be visible on a selection display. Depending on the particular aid, the items that are stored can be programmable (created by or for a particular individual) or preprogrammed (unable to be changed except by the manufacturer).[3]

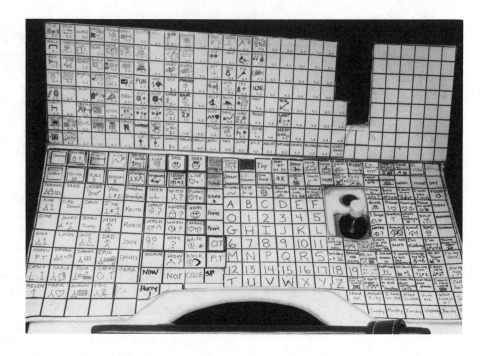

FIGURE 12-3. Use of a code to increase the number of available vocabulary items beyond what can be placed directly on the selection display. (Photo by Corbit's Studio, Bridgeport, CT.)

COMPARING NONELECTRONIC WITH ELECTRONIC ENCODING

When encoding is used with a nonelectronic aid, the partner must be able to understand and decipher the code the individual is indicating. This means that, in selecting code elements, the partner must be considered as well as the individual who will be using the code. It is possible that more than one code may have to be developed if all partners cannot understand the same code. Some partners may not be able to use any code at all.

When an electronic encoding aid is used that produces spoken or printed output, the aid translates the code into a spoken or printed message so that the partner does not have to understand the code itself. This removes the responsibility of deciphering messages from the partner and eliminates the possibility of confusing or forgetting codes. It also gives the individual greater independence in producing messages and increases the number of people with whom communication is possible.

USING ABBREVIATIONS TO REMEMBER CODES

Along with the ability to store a great number of items in an electronic aid comes the problem of remembering a great number of codes. If code elements have some relationship to the item being stored, they may be easier to remember. For example, if letters of the alphabet are used as encoding elements, abbreviations can be assigned to stored words. This may be easier for the individual to learn and remember than codes such as numbers that have no relationship to the corresponding item; e.g., the letters *T-V* to stand for "I want to watch TV" are easier to remember than the number code *1-3*.

The technique of using abbreviations as codes is called *abbreviation/expansion* because the aid expands the abbreviation into a completely spelled message. SpeechPAC is an example of a portable computer-based aid that uses this technique. It allows the user to assign two or three letter combinations, or abbreviations, to stored items through Logical Letter Coding (LOLEC); e.g., "I want a cup of coffee" can be assigned the logical letter code *W-C-C*. When the abbreviation for an item is selected, the aid expands it into an entire word or phrase. Although the individual initially may need to refer to a chart displaying these codes and their corresponding items, eventually, the codes can be memorized more easily than if unrelated letters were used.

MORSE CODE

A system that can be used with an encoding technique for individuals who can spell is Morse code. This is a system of dots and dashes that stand for the letters of the alphabet, numerals, and punctuation. When used with an unaided technique, the individual can produce the dots and dashes through any body part under which there is some control; e.g., one eye blink for a dot, two blinks for a dash. The partner must then translate these dots and dashes into letters. When used with an electronic aid, these dots and dashes can be produced with the same single or multiple swithes used with scanning aids. The electronic aid then translates the code into printed or spoken letters, numbers, and punctuation. With most aids, words and phrases can also be assigned codes not used in the formal Morse code system.

Morse code can greatly increase rate of communication for those individuals with limited physical control by reducing the range of motion required over direct selection and decreasing the time from that required by scanning.[3] Because items are produced by the user rather than selected from a display, when paired with speech output, it can be used by individuals with visual impairments, who could not see a display.

Using Morse code requires sufficient physical ability to produce the dots and dashes and sufficient cognitive and linguistic ability to be able to translate the code into movement. However, for those with the ability to use it, Morse code is much easier to learn than even a very small number of words in a foreign language.[3]

When using an encoding aid, regardless of the specific code elements used, most individuals initiallly will need to refer to a chart to remember the codes and the words they correspond to. Eventually, most individuals memorize a large number, if not all, of the items.

In designing a chart that corresponds to codes used with an electronic aid, there is often a problem as to where to display it without interfering with the use of the aid or the partner's view of it, if a visual display or printer is used. One solution is to incorporate the individual's nonelectronic aid into the chart.

Figure 12-4 shows an individual who uses SpeechPAC and a nonelectronic aid consisting of words, phrases, and the alphabet. All the items on the nonelectronic aid have been stored in SpeechPAC, and each item on the nonelectronic aid is labeled with the letter code assigned to it. A space is left on the nonelectronic display for the SpeechPAC. This space displays the letters of the alphabet, which are unnecessary when using the SpeechPAC, since the individual has access to them on the aid's keyboard. This arrangement provides the individual with a chart upon which the coded items are displayed and access to both nonelectronic and electronic aids at the same time.

While this idea will not work for everyone, the idea of incorporating the chart with the indivdual's nonelectronic aid may have great applicability. For example, to learn Morse code, the code corresponding to each letter can be placed on the individual's nonelectronic alphabet board. This can be especially useful in the early stages of training, when the individual is still unfamiliar with it.

FIGURE 12-4. A nonelectronic aid used in conjunction with SpeechPAC. (Photo by Corbit's Studio.)

While codes can be displayed for the user to refer to, the chart they are displayed upon may become large and cumbersome. In addition, some individuals may have great difficulty referring to a chart and may also have difficulty memorizing or using a code.

A technique that can alleviate this problem is the use of levels, where each square on a selection display contains several items rather than only one item. Each item is assigned to a different level.

Vois 135 is an example of an electronic aid that uses levels. Figure 12-5 shows this aid used with two levels. Each target area is divided in half. Words in the lower half are in black, indicating the item is stored in Level 3, while words in the upper half are in red, indicating that the item is stored in Level 4. In order to produce an item in Level 3, the individual first activates the target labeled *Level 3*, then activates the target containing the desired item. Because the items and their levels are displayed on the aid itself, the need for the user to memorize codes is eliminated.

This technique is only useful to the extent that more than one item can be displayed in a square. There may be several reasons why this cannot be done. The individual may have visual problems and cannot see items that are printed or drawn very small, necessitating that only one item be placed in a square. Another reason is that the square itself may be so small that only one item can be printed or drawn in it, yet be recognizable to the individual. A third reason may be that, in order to recognize an item, the individual may require a picture or symbol instead of or in addition to a printed word, which would take up the entire space of a square. In any of these cases, levels usually cannot be used.[4]

FIGURE 12-5. The Vois 135 used with two levels.

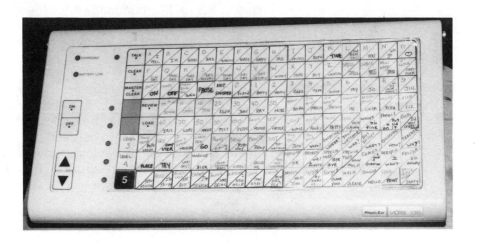

MODIFYING ENCODING ELEMENTS USED WITH ELECTRONIC AIDS

Very often, although an individual can physically control a particular electronic aid, it is not considered because he or she cannot functionally use the encoding elements that the manufacturer intended to be used with the aid. For example, an aid that uses letter elements may be eliminated for an individual who cannot spell or an aid that uses number elements may be eliminated for an individual who cannot do arithmetic.

However, although many aids use letters or numbers as code elements, it is not necessary that an individual be able to spell or do arithmetic to use them. The individual who can match code elements to their corresponding items can use those elements; e.g., in order to use letters as code elements, the individual only needs to know how to match letters.[3]

If an individual cannot match the code elements used by an electronic aid, the elements can be replaced. For example, the SpeechPAC aid, described earlier, has a keyboard with numbers and letters on it. If an individual cannot match letters, stickers can be pasted on the keys displaying the code elements that the individual can use; e.g., different colored stickers on the right side of the panel and different shaped stickers on the left. When asked for a code by the aid, any combination of colors and shapes can be pushed. When asked for the expansion (the message to be stored), the word or phrase is typed in. To call the item back, the individual just has to press the sequence of colors and shapes. As far as the aid is concerned, it is simply looking at the sequence of keys or squares being indicated and does not care whether there are letters, shapes, number, or colors on those keys. The aid will print letters on the visual screen and printer but not the colors or pictures used as coding elements on the panel.[3]

Thus, if an individual can physically control a particular aid that meets his or her communication needs, but cannot use the coding elements available with it, these elements can be modified. The choice of encoding elements is entirely up to the clinician.

MINSPEAK

Although encoding elements can be modified for a particular individual as just described, a code based upon shapes and colors or letters and numbers may be difficult to learn and memorize because of the lack of relationship between the code and the item it represents. MINSPEAK, also called *semantic compaction*, uses a sequence of icons or symbols to express meanings. These icons, shown on the selection display of an aid, can represent a variety of meanings. The meaning of an icon in a MINSPEAK system is determined by the other icons used with it. For example, the meaning of an icon illustrating a house can mean a bank when used with an icon showing a dollar bill, while the same house icon used with a glass of liquid can mean a bar. MINSPEAK is presently implemented through two electronic aids, Touch Talker and Light Talker, so that when an icon code is selected, the message it represents is spoken, displayed, or printed.[5]

A MINSPEAK user can use 50 or 60 icons in thousands of different combinations. Although a standard set of icons designed for MINSPEAK is available with suggested meanings, MINSPEAK users can design their own icons and assign their own meanings. A program allows the user or others to type in the vocabulary items that each icon code represents and store it in the aid's memory. To retrieve a desired item, the user selects the assigned icon code.[5]

Figure 12-6 shows a standard MINSPEAK display as it is implemented through Touch Talker. An icon has been assigned to a number of the target areas on the aid's selection display. The particular user of this aid has decided that the sun icon stands for greetings. When paired with the question icon, this stands for "Good morning. How are you?" When the sun is paired with the icon for eye, which can stand for *I*, this stands for "Hello. My name is Jessica."

Thus, rather than assigning a vocabulary item a code consisting of letters, numbers, or other elements, the code meaning is assigned by the user. Because the codes are easier to recall, the individual can remember and use a larger number of coded sentences.[3]

FIGURE 12-6. A MINSPEAK display. (Photo by Corbit's Studio.) Used with permission from the Prentke Romich Company, Wooster, OH.)

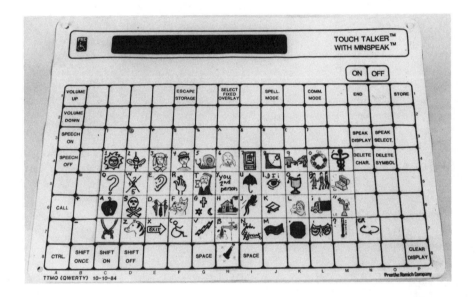

REFERENCES

1. Harris, D., & Vanderheiden, G. (1980). Enhancing the development of communicative interaction. In R. L. Schiefelbusch (Ed.), *Nonspeech language and communication: Analysis and intervention* (pp. 268–269). Baltimore: University Park Press.

2. Vanderheiden, G. C. (1977). Providing the child with a means to indicate. In G. C. Vanderheiden and K. Grilley (Eds.), *Non-vocal communication techniques and aids for the severely physically handicapped*. (pp. 49–51). Baltimore: University Park Press.

3. Vanderheiden, G. (1986). Personal communication.

4. Vanderheiden, G. & Lloyd, L. (in press). *Communication systems and their components. In S. W. Blackstone (Ed.), Augmentative communication: An introduction*. Rockville, MD: American Speech and Hearing Association.

5. Baker, B. (1985). The use of words and phrases on a MINSPEAK communication system. *Communication Outlook*, 7(1), 8–9.

13

Control Switches Used with Electronic Aids

TYPES OF SWITCHES

Electronic scanning, directed scanning, and certain encoding techniques must be controlled through a switch, which acts as an interface between the individual and the aid. Most switches used with communication aids are operated through momentary contact; that is, the switch is normally open. When activated through some means, the switch is closed. As soon as the activating force is removed, the switch returns to the open condition.[1] Each switch accommodates different physical abilities through its method of activation and its physical design.

These switches are generally activated through direct exertion of pressure by the individual. The switch is usually placed off the body of the user who must then move toward it in order to activate it in some manner.

The most common type of switch activated through pressure is a tread or paddle switch, of which there are many variations. It is usually activated by depressing the paddle, a flat area, which remains activated until pressure is released (Fig. 13-1). Another variation is a plate switch, which provides a large flat surface area (or plate) that is activated by touching any part of its surface (Fig. 13-2).

The design of a tread switch accommodates those with gross movement of any body part: an arm, chin, elbow, knee. An audible click or physical spring of the action in the switch may be provided to let the user know that the switch has been actuated and released. The actuating area may be of contrasting color to the body of the switch or a bright color to provide a visible target.

There are many variations of pressure switches designed to be used with specific control sites or by those with certain physical abilities. For example, the lever switch was developed for activation through side-to-side head motion (Fig. 13-3) and works by activating a round surface, covered with a spongelike material, that is attached to a rod. Since

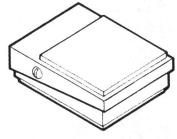

FIGURE 13-1. A tread switch activated by exerting pressure. (Drawing courtesy of ZYGO Industries, Inc., Portland, OR.)

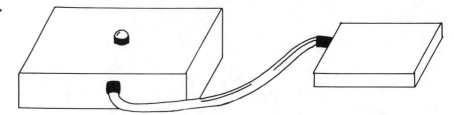

FIGURE 13-2. A plate switch▶ connected to a buzzer. (Drawing by Ava Barber, New York, NY, adapted from a drawing by Arroyo and Associates, Inc., Glendale, NY.)

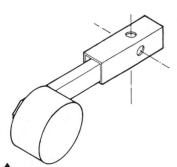

▲ **FIGURE 13-3.** A lever switch developed for side-to-side head motion. (Drawing courtesy of ZYGO Industries, Inc.)

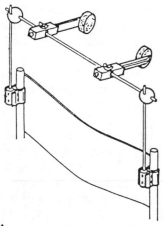

▲ **FIGURE** **13-4.** Wheelchair mounting system for a lever switch. (Drawing courtesy of ZYGO Industries, Inc.)

FIGURE 13-5. A cushion switch▶ (manufactured by Arroyo and Assocs, Inc.) with a buzzer. (Photo by Corbit's Studio, Bridgeport, CT.)

the user may not be able to see the switch, because it is placed at the side of the head, the switch provides clear auditory and tactile feedback through its snap action. Because it is intended to be activated with the head, it is also designed to be easily mounted to a variety of wheelchair configurations, bed frames, etc. (Fig. 13-4).

Another pressure-sensitive switch is a "puff and sip" switch, which involves blowing into (puffing) or sucking from (sipping) a tube placed near the mouth. Displacement of the air in the tube activates the switch.[1] This requires breath control, rather than respiratory control, so that the switch can be used by an individual with respiratory difficulties. It also requires good lip closure and lip control so that this type of switch is frequently used by quadriplegic, spinal-cord-injured individuals who have intact oral musculature.

Pressure switches are also used with cushion (squeeze-bulb) switches. When the cushions are pressed, air is forced through the pressure switch. Cushion switches are softer than plate or tread switches and, so, may be more comfortably activated by those who exert a great amount of pressure (Fig. 13-5)[1]

Pressure switches are usually placed off the body of the user, who must move toward the switch in order to activate it. When a switch is placed off the body, the user must be positioned well enough to allow

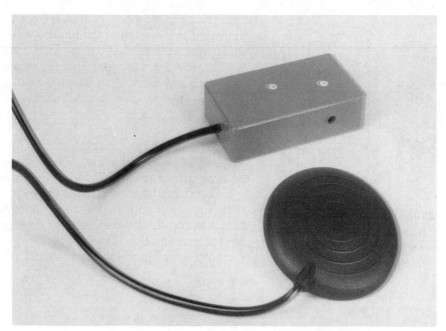

ELECTRONIC COMMUNICATION AIDS

movement toward the switch in order to apply sufficient pressure. The switch must also be mounted so that the individual can activate it independently. If the switch is held by someone else, the individual will not have independent control of the aid. The person holding the switch cannot help but move closer or further away as the switch is activated, which will further diminish the individual's control. Thus, it will never be clear who is controlling the aid: the individual or the person holding the switch.

In addition to activation by pressure, there are switches that can be activated by almost any muscle movement. An example of this is the P-switch (Fig. 13-6), named for the piezoelectric sensor it uses. Piezoelectric elements convert movements into electrical signals. The electronics of the P-switch, housed in a shirt pocket-size package, receive these electrical signals when the user moves.

The piezoelectric sensor, about the size of a quarter, is held in place with a soft velcro strap. With a pair of scissors, this strap can be made into a headband to sense brow motion, a bracelet to sense wrist motion, a ring to sense the motion of a finger, etc. The P-switch, however, is triggered by relative motion; the actual position of the sensor is unimportant.[2]

Thus, when a switch, such as the P-switch, is placed on the user's body, activation is far less dependent on the user's position since the control site activating the switch remains in the same relationship to the switch no matter how the user is positioned. The problems with placing a switch on the user's body is to ensure that the position is comfortable to the user and that the switch will stay in position without constant adjustment by someone else.

FIGURE 13-6. The P-switch sensor mounted on a headband. (Drawing courtesy of ETI Corporation, Lansing, MI.)

USING SINGLE AND MULTIPLE SWITCHES WITH DIFFERENT CONTROL TECHNIQUES

Electronic linear and row-column scanning aids are controlled by a single switch. With linear scanning, activation of the switch will move the indicator from one target to the next or stop the indicator from moving from one target to the next. With row-column scanning, activation of the switch will change the pattern of movement of the indicator from row to column, from column to indication of the selected item, or from indicating the item back to row scanning.

Directed scanning aids are controlled by mulitple switches: either a small array of single switches or a joystick. In a small array of single switches, each switch controls a different direction of movement of an indicator; when one switch is activated, it causes the indicator to move to the right, another causes it to move to the left, etc. An example of a small array of switches used for directed scanning is an arm slot control (Fig. 13-7), which consists of five deeply recessed tread switches. Each of four switches moves an indicator in a different direction. The fifth switch is used as a call signal.

A joystick is a switch capable of moving in several different directions by pushing the stick. This controls the direction of movement of an indicator on an aid's display. Joysticks are capable of moving in many different directions, but those used with communication aids typically move in four directions (Fig. 13-8).

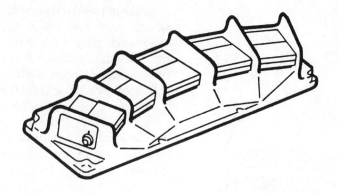

FIGURE 13-7. An arm slot control consisting of five single switches. (Drawing courtesy of ZYGO Industries, Inc.)

FIGURE 13-8. A joystick capable of moving in four directions. (Drawing courtesy of ZYGO Industries, Inc.)

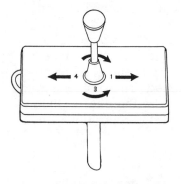

In addition to directed scanning aids, electronic aids using encoding techniques also can be controlled through multiple switches, each switch sending a different code to the aid. For example, when using Morse code, several types of switches can be used:

1. Two single switches, one producing a "dit" and the other producing a "dah," each placed at different control sites. For example, a lever switch can be placed on either side of an individual's head.
2. A single switch capable of producing a "dit" when activated at one end and a "dah" when activated at another.
3. A single switch capable of sending a "dit" or a "dah" through the duration at which the switch is activated.

When multiple switches are used, an additional switch can be used to produce an enter signal, so that the individual has a chance to correct an item before it is entered.

SELECTING SWITCHES

Among electronic aids, there is great flexibility in the selection of a particular switch to control the aid. Basically, the switch should be matched to the individual's abilities rather than requiring him to struggle to control a particular switch.

In selecting a control site, it is important that activation of the switch is not restricted to certain body parts; e.g., a tread switch to be activated only with a hand. Rather, a number of control sites should be explored; although, as discussed previously, some switches are designed to be activated more easily with certain body parts than with others.

An important feature to consider in selecting switches is the feedback the switch provides to the user to signal when the switch is activated. Feedback can be provided through visual, auditory, and tactile channels. For example, the individual who activates the switch may be able to see it move, may hear it click, and feel it react to pressure. The more feedback the switch gives to the individual, the more it helps him or her to accurately control it.

ELECTRONIC COMMUNICATION AIDS

SUBSTITUTING AND STANDARDIZING SWITCHES

Most aids are manufactured with several different switch options, which allow for differences in physical ability among users. Functionally similar switches made for different aids can usually be interchanged because of increased standardization of cable connectors and electrical characteristics used by manufacturers. This gives the individual greater flexibility in selecting switches.[1]

However, not all manufacturers use the same standard connectors; so, sometimes, a functionally similar switch cannot be used with an aid. In such a case, some adaptation must be made to the connectors between the switch and the aid, either through the purchase of a common connector or through the services of a rehabilitation engineer.

Lack of standardization requires extra time and money to locate and purchase connectors. It can also result in damaged equipment if the electrical characteristics of a switch and an aid are incompatible. Standard interface specifications for connectors and electrical requirements, developed by the Trace Research and Development Center on Communication, Control and Computer Access for Handicapped Individuals, in Madison, Wisconsin, are being complied with by many manufacturers, so that lack of compatability will become less of a problem.[1]

USING ONE SWITCH TO CONTROL MANY DEVICES

In addition to many switches capable of controlling one aid, one switch can control many devices if the devices can be controlled by a functionally similar switch. Such devices may include an attention-getting buzzer, an environmental control unit, a computer, adapted toys, etc. Ideally, once a control site is located and the best switch controlled by that site is found, the switch can be used for multiple functions.

However, the individual who needs to perform two functions at once may need two switches controlled by different control sites. For example, a child playing with an adapted toy also may need the ability to call for attention, so two switches, one for the buzzer and for the toy, will be needed. It may be necessary that two different switches be used if the individual has different physical ability with each control site. For example, a lever switch may be needed to use the head as a control site and a tread switch to use the hand. The exception to this would be if the device could perform the two functions (e.g., a communication aid with a built-in attention-getting alarm that the individual could select through its display).

DECIDING TO BUY OR TO MAKE SWITCHES

Because funding is always a concern, the question often arises of whether it is more cost efficient to buy switches or make them. At many facilities, a large part of equipment budget is spent on purchasing commercially available switches; while at others, clinicians make the switches used by their clients.

A decision as to whether to make or buy switches must be based, in part, upon the total cost of the switch over a period of time. Although homemade switches may initially cost less, they may end up costing more than if bought. Commercially available switches designed by rehabilitation engineers are designed to be durable—to be dropped, drooled upon, etc. Homemade switches may not be as durable and, so, have a higher repair rate, requiring clinician time for the repairs. The time it takes for a clinician to make a switch and to repair it may equal the amount it costs to purchase a more durable, reliable switch.

In addition, the ease with which a switch can be used must also be considered. The design features of commercially available switches cannot be easily or inexpensively emulated. Switch manufacturers may spend years designing special features to accommodate different physical abilities, including sensitivity to pressure, mountability, size, shape, materials, and feedback to the user upon activation. Homemade switches rarely have all these features and, as a result, may not be as easily controlled. Thus, the homemade switch may be more difficult for the individual to control than a commercially available one.

If a facility or individual is able to make a homemade switch that can be reliably and easily controlled, it should be used. Rather than using switches from one source, however, a combination of homemade and commercially available switches would probably be the most efficient solution. This would allow those individuals who need switches with specific design features not provided by homemade switches to have them. It would also allow the homemade switches to be used by those individuals who could control them. In some cases, an individual could use a homemade switch for one function (e.g., attention-getting) and a commercially available switch for another (e.g., controlling a communication aid).

REFERENCES

1. Gunderson, J. R. (1985). Interfacing the motor impaired. In J. G. Webster, et al. (Eds.), *Electronic devices for rehabilitation*. New York: John Wiley & Sons.
2. News on aids. (1986). *Communication Outlook*, Vol. 7, No. 4, 15.

PART V

Symbols, Vocabulary Items, and Vocabulary Capabilities

DEFINING TERMS

Selecting symbols that are appropriate to an individual's needs and abilities to communicate is a crucial consideration in providing an effective communication aid. Of equal importance to selecting symbols, however, is selecting appropriate vocabulary items (the thoughts and ideas the individual wants to express) that are represented by symbols. An individual who cannot spell is dependent on others to provide vocabulary items for his or her selection. Even an individual who can spell will still need words and phrases in addition to the alphabet. Spelling each word, letter by letter, can be quite slow, but if a whole word can be pointed to, the number of movements needed to produce the word is decreased. Both spellers and nonspellers also will need items to help control and clarify conversation and to repair misunderstandings when they occur.

In addition to selecting vocabulary items and symbols, the vocabulary capabilities of the communication aid must also be considered. This refers to the capability of the aid to display or store items chosen by or for a particular individual and to allow modification as needed.

Thus, in order for a communication aid to be used successfully, the vocabulary capabilities of the aid, the selected vocabulary items, and the symbols representing these items must match the individual's communication needs and abilities.

14

Symbols Used with Communication Aids

TYPES OF SYMBOLS MOST FREQUENTLY USED

Graphic symbols can be written or drawn then placed on a selection display or stored in the memory of a communication aid. The symbols most frequently used are traditional orthography and pictographs.

Traditional orthography refers to regular printed letters of the alphabet. Using this system, the individual can create any word he or she knows how to spell. Other forms of traditional orthography are Morse code, braille, and finger spelling, which allow individuals with various physical impairments access to traditional orthography. They also include modified alphabets with a 1:1 phonetic correspondence between spoken and written letters.

A pictograph represents the meaning of a word or concept through a picture; e.g., a photograph, picture, or line drawing of a house to represent *house*. Use of pictographs alone limits access to language to those items available to the individual with the aid. When ideographic and arbitrary symbols also are used, more abstract concepts can be represented. An ideograph represents an idea related to the word; e.g., a drawing of an apple to represent *hunger*. An arbitrary symbol is one to which meaning is assigned; e.g., Blissymbols uses the symbol / to represent *the*.[1]

CONSIDERATIONS IN SELECTING SYMBOLS

One dimension that must be considered in selecting symbols is openness. Traditional orthography is highly open because the user can express any item that can be spelled. In contrast, pictographs have more limited openness, since they do not provide access to any words or concepts beyond those displayed on the aid.[2] As mentioned previously, those pictographic systems that incorporate ideographic and abstract symbols tend to be more open than those that use only pictures, since it is difficult to represent abstract concepts through pictures alone.

However, the more open a symbol system is, the more abstract it is, e.g., printed words are highly abstract symbols, bearing no relationship to the concepts they represent while letters of the alphabet have only a loose phonetic relationship to the spoken language.[2] This makes the system more difficult to learn than one that is closely related to its referents.

Thus, symbols must be chosen that will provide the openness the individual needs but that also are within his or her cognitive/linguistic abilities.

Another dimension to be considered is the intelligibility of the symbols: the ability of the symbol to be understood with no prior training. This depends on the output of the aid and the obviousness of the symbols.[2]

With an electronic aid, the need for the partner to understand the symbols the individual is using depends upon the output produced. For example, if the aid produces speech output, the partner does not have to understand the particular symbols used, since the message needs only to be listened to rather than interpreted. If the aid produces printed output, the partner need not know the specific symbols but must know how to read.

With a nonelectronic aid, the obviousness of the symbols used is important because the partner must combine them into a message as the individual indicates them. If an alphabet is used, the partner must know how to read. If a pictograph is used, the word or phrase corresponding to it should be printed above it because the meaning of the symbol generally is not obvious to those unfamiliar with the system.[2] For example, a picture of a house could indicate the individual's house, a house he visits, or any building. A partner who is unable to read the word printed above the symbol must understand the specific system being used.

If a pictographic system is used that allows the individual to create new words not displayed on the aid through the use of strategies, printing the word corresponding to the symbols would not be of assistance. For example, using Blissymbols, the word *talk* can be created by indicating *action* then *mouth*. In such a case, the partner would have to know that strategy in order to understand the message.

In selecting symbols, the time available to train the partner to learn symbols also must be considered. If the individual will be communicating with unfamiliar partners or partners with very little time available, then symbols easily intelligible to an untrained person must be used.

Thus, with different partners, symbols from different sources may be used depending upon the partners' abilities. For example, to communicate through a nonelectronic aid with a young child who cannot read, the speech-impaired individual will need pictographs. Symbols that are highly obvious to the child may be chosen over ones that will take more time to train the young partner to understand. When communicating with his nurse, however, the individual can use traditional orthography.

Because extensive time can be involved in choosing different symbols for use with different partners, many speech-impaired individuals are limited in those with whom they can communicate. For example, speech-impaired children using nonelectronic aids often cannot communicate with their speaking peers, who do not understand the symbols the child is using.

PICTOGRAPHS, BLISSYMBOLS, AND PICSYMS

Pictographs include photographs, line drawings, and pictures from magazines, books, etc. They all have a very close relationship to their referents but vary in their degree of openness and intelligibility. For example, the word *house* can be represented by a photo of the individual's house, a picture from a magazine advertisement, or a line drawing of a house.

Pictographs can consist of a set of pictures and/or photos for each idea to be represented, gathered or created by the person designing the aid. Prepackaged sets of drawings and photos also can be purchased, available in several sizes and designed to depict a variety of meanings. These sets eliminate the need for looking for specific pictures or drawing them. They also give the clinician a standard set of pictures that can be used to make duplicate boards or to use with several individuals.[2] Examples from one prepackaged set are illustrated in Figure 14-1.

Photographs and hand-drawn symbols allow the individual's vocabulary to be expanded in any direction or to include any concept within the creative abilities of those working with him or her. Prepackaged sets are easier to use but tend to limit the topics or specific symbol choices to those provided in the set. In general, any aids using preprinted symbols should also use custom-drawn symbols to expand and individualize the displays to meet the specific needs of the user.[2]

In addition to pictographic symbol sets, there are symbol systems specifically designed to incorporate strategies that allow maximum communication and to be maximally open in terms of ideas that can be expressed. Since there are only a limited number of ways to draw objects that are easily represented by pictographs, the similarity among sets and among sets and systems is more striking than their differences. The major difference between prepackaged symbol sets and symbol systems is how to represent objects, actions, etc., that are not easily represented by pictures.[2] Different approaches to this problem have been taken by various standardized systems, two of which will be discussed. For further discussion of symbol systems, the reader is referred to the sources listed at the end of this chapter.

FIGURE 14-1. Examples of symbols from PCS (Picture Communication Symbols), a prepackaged symbol set. (Picture Communication Symbols, (1981), Mayer-Johnson Company, Stillwater, Minnesota. Used with permission.)

Blissymbols

santa claus

santa claus

santa claus

FIGURE 14-2. Blissymbols that can be used to represent "Santa Claus." Markings around the symbols indicate that no standard symbol exists. (Blissymbolics used herein derived from the symbols described in the work, **Semantography**, original copyright © C.K. Bliss, 1949. Blissymbolics Communication Institute, Exclusive licensee, 1982.)

FIGURE 14-3. Use of the Blissymbol action indicator. When the action indicator is placed above the symbol for "mouth," the symbol stands for "talk" or "speak." (Blissymbolics used herein derived from the symbols described in the work, *Semantography*, original copyright © C.K. Bliss, 1949.) Blissymbolics Communication Institute, Exclusive licensee, 1982.)

Blissymbols originally were developed as an international communication system by Charles Bliss, a linguist. It later was applied by the Ontario Crippled Children's Centre as a symbol system for speech-impaired children who were unable to spell.[3]

Blissymbols were designed to communicate the maximum amount of information with a minimum number of symbols and concepts. The set consists of a core vocabulary of 100 symbols, which include pictographs as well as ideographic and arbitrary symbols. Mixed symbols consist of a combination of all three types.

Blissymbols tend to be meaning-shaped and to depict the general concept rather than specific features. For example, the Blissymbol for Santa Claus can consist of the symbols for *man* and *Christmas* (Fig. 14-2), rather than a drawing of Santa Claus. It can also consist of *man/big/stomach* or *father/Christmas*. There is no standard symbol for Santa Claus at this time.

The system is also designed to enhance openness through combining the symbols provided with strategies and indicators. For example, when the action indicator is placed above the symbol for mouth, the symbol stands for *talk* or *speak* (Fig. 14-3). This gives the individual access to words not displayed on or stored in the aid.

In order to keep the system highly standardized among users, Blissymbols have specific guidelines for drawing existing symbols or creating new ones. Stamp sets, stickers, stencils, and other materials can be purchased to assist in creating displays.

Standardization and consistency amongst Blissymbol users enables them to communicate with each other. Using Blissymbols consistently with one individual rather than using symbols from several sources also can facilitate learning the system.

Individuals who are unable to spell often are able to learn to use Blissymbols more easily because they are primarily meaning-based. Dyslexic reading problems may not interfere with the ability to use Blissymbols to the degree that they interfere with using traditional orthography. Users who were unable to read often acquire a sight vocabulary just through frequent exposure to the English words printed with the Blissymbols they use.[3]

Because of the relatively simple line shapes of Blissymbols, they are easily written by hand or displayed or printed with computers. As a result, Blissymbols can be used as a written pictographic form of communication.

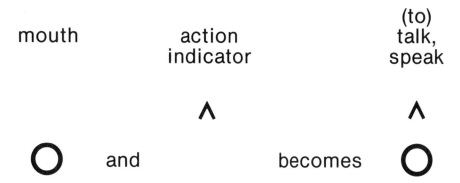

Picsyms

FIGURE 14-4. Picsym symbol for "Santa Claus." (Reprinted from PICSYMS Categorical Dictionary, written and illustrated by Faith Carlson, copyright 1985, Baggeboda Press, Lawrence, KS.)

USING ONE SYMBOL GRAPHIC SET OR SYSTEM VERSUS SEVERAL

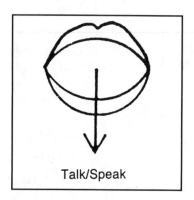

FIGURE 14-5. Picsym symbol for "talk." (Reprinted from PICSYMS Categorical Dictionary, written and illustrated by Faith Carlson, copyright 1985, Baggeboda Press, Lawrence, KS.)

Picsyms is a pictographic symbol system designed by Faith Carlson specifically to be used by individuals who use communication aids. Picsyms provide a system for creating and using symbols for a particular individual. It includes materials and instruction on how to create recognizable and usable pictographic symbols whenever they are needed. Symbols drawn by the user or the clinician can supplement the predrawn symbols to expand and customize the individual's vocabulary.[4]

The approach differs from that of Blissymbols in that symbols are created using the distinctive characteristics of the referent. For example, to represent Santa Claus, the most distinctive characteristics of Santa Claus would be used to create the symbol (Fig. 14-4). This is in contrast to the Blissymbol representation, which depicts the concepts involved with Santa Claus rather than the actual features.

However, the approach is similar to Blissymbols in that consistent strategies and indicators are used to expand vocabulary. In the previous example with Blissymbols, an action indicator above a symbol indicates an action: e.g., *talk* is formed from combining *mouth* and the *action indicator*. With Picsyms, a simple arrow shape indicates action. To represent *talk* a picture of a mouth with an arrow coming out of it is used (Fig. 14-5).

One advantage of using a single set or system for symbols is that if many individuals in the immediate environment also use it, they will understand each others symbols and can communicate with each other. When only a few individuals use one set or system, the advantage would be limited.[2] In addition, if a specific system is used, the individual may be able to achieve the maximum degree of openness by using the strategies and symbols of that system consistently rather than mixing various sets and systems.

The disadvantage of using one source is that, if a symbol from a particular set or system is too abstract for the user or not obvious enough for partners to understand, the individual may not be able to use it. Another disadvantage is that, if the set or system is limited in openness, the individual is limited in the ideas that could be expressed.

Thus, hand-drawn pictographs or those collected from magazines and photos, prepackaged sets of pictographic symbols, and symbol systems can be combined to represent each vocabulary item. New symbols can be created incorporating ideas from different sources as well.

TRADITIONAL ORTHOGRAPHY AND RELATED SYSTEMS

Traditional orthography allows an individual to express an unlimited number of ideas using a small number of subsymbols: 26 letters. This makes the individual's access to language limited only by his or her ability to spell, not by the items displayed on or stored in the aid. Traditional orthography also generally is understood by a large number of people. Therefore, it is the best system for speech-impaired individuals but, as was discussed previously, it is also more abstract and so more difficult to learn than pictographic symbols.

Spelling should not be overlooked as a system for individuals who have limited spelling ability. Misspelled words still can be understood, although the spelling must be close enough to be intelligible to the partner. Additionally, words need not always be spelled in their entirety, as partners invariably predict many words through context. Giving the first letter of a word, which places even less demands on spelling skills, can be used as a supplemental strategy for individuals whose speech is limited in intelligibility. Accurate spelling skills are desirable, however, because the more accurate is the individual's spelling, the more people he or she can communicate with, despite their lack of familiarity with his or her particular spelling pattern.

Using Whole Words and Phrases with the Alphabet

Spelling messages letter by letter can be extremely slow. In contrast with a normal rate of spoken English of approximately 180 words per minute, communication rate when pointing to individual letters on an alphabet board is limited to approximately 2–8 words per minute.[5] Individuals using scanning or encoding systems to spell messages require even more time.

Communication rate can be increased by reducing the number of movements required to produce a word. This can be done by providing words and phrases, chosen by their frequency of use, because each item will increase communication rate only when it is selected. In addition, frequently used letter combinations can be selected. WRITE is a system specifically developed using this idea[6] and incorporates frequently occurring letter groupings: have, they, you, etc. (Fig. 14-6).

Strategies to help clarify words that are being spelled should also be included. For example, strategies are needed to indicate a space between each new word and to indicate when the individual is going to start over due to a mistake in spelling, to modify the message, or because the partner misunderstood a word. Figure 14-7 shows an example of an alphabet board with these strategies. Additionally, words that assist in maintaining conversational control need to be included; this will be discussed further in Chapter 15.

a	about	ac	ad	h	ha	had	n	n't	nd	t	ta	te	ter		
al	all	an	and	have	he	her	ne	ng	ni	th	that	that's	the		
any	ar	are	as	here	hi	ho	no	not	nt	them	then	there	they	1	2
at	b	ba	be	i	i'm	if	o	of	oh	on	they're	thing	think	3	4
because	bo	but	c	il	in	ing	one	or	other	out	this	ti	time	5	6
ca	can	ce	ch	ion	ir	is	p	pa	pe	to	too	ty	u	7	8
ci	ck	co	could	It	it's	j	just	people	pl	ugh	un	up	ur	9	10
course	ct	d	day	k	ke	ki	know	qu	r	us	ut	v	ve	0	SPACE
de	di	do	don't	l	la	le	ra	re	really	w	wa	ver	vi	.	,
down	e	ed	el	li	like	little	ri	ro	rt	was	way	we	well	?	...
en	er	es	f	ll	lo	ly	ry	s	sa	says	were	what	when	!	
fa	fe	fi	for	m	ma	me	school	se	see	sh	wi	with	work	'	's
from	g	ge	get	mean	mi	mo	she	si	so	some	would	x	y		
ght	go	going	good	got	much	my	ss	st	sta	su	yeah	year	you	z	

FIGURE 14-6. An example of a WRITE display. (Courtesy of Tufts-New England Medical Center.)

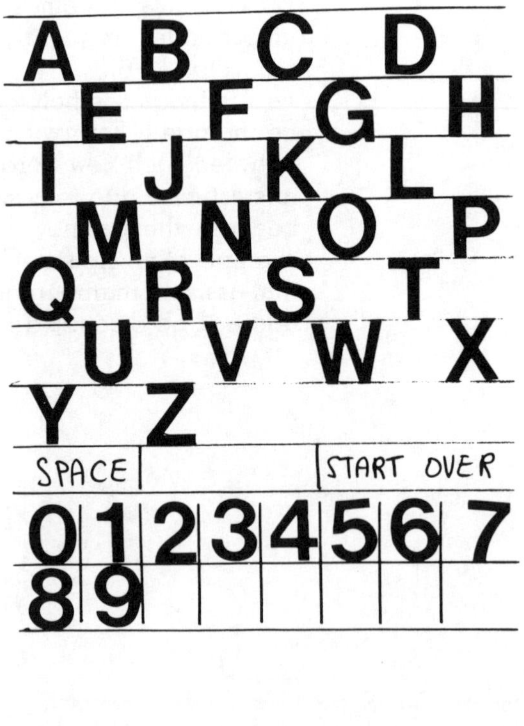

FIGURE 14-7. Alphabet board with the strategies "SPACE" and "START OVER." (Photo by Corbit's Studio, Bridgeport, CT.)

ELECTRONIC COMMUNICATION AIDS

SPELLING VOCABULARY ITEMS WITH ELECTRONIC AIDS PRODUCING SPEECH OUTPUT

With electronic aids using text-to-speech, the individual spells a word that is produced in its entirety by the speech output of the aid. For example, if the letters *H-E-L-L-O* are selected, the word *hello* will be spoken.

Different types of text-to-speech programs are used with different electronic aids. Each program has its own spelling rules and requires some modification in spelling so that the words are pronounced correctly. For example, the word *typewriter* will be pronounced "tip writer" with one particular text-to-speech program. When spelled with a hyphen (*type-writer*), it is pronounced correctly.

This is due to the set of rules programmed to enable the speech synthesizer to convert the printed word into a spoken word. Most words fall into this program, but written English does not always correspond to its spoken form—as anyone trying to learn English can testify. In the case of *typewriter*, the synthesizer pronounces the entry *t-y-p-e*, which is a consonent-*y*-consonant-*e*-consonant combination, with a short *i* as in tip. This works well for such words as *pyramid* or *synthesis* but not for *typewriter*.

The use of text-to-speech requires knowledge of spelling and the ability to modify it according to the rules of the synthesizer, in order to produce intelligible words. In certain cases, its use may be limited to those with accurate spelling ability. In other cases, an individual may find it easier to learn the spelling/pronunciation rules of a particular synthesizer than to learn traditional spelling.

Some electronic aids now can be programmed to pronounce a word correctly even though it is not spelled according to the aid's pronunciation rules. In the example just discussed, if the individual spells *typewriter* without the hyphen, the aid can be programmed to pronounce it correctly. However, for this to be effective, the programmer must be able to predict which words the individual cannot spell according to the synthesizer's rules and how they will be spelled, in order to program them into the aid's memory. The individual also must be consistent in spelling the words the way the aid has been programmed to accept them.

In addition to using traditional orthography to spell words, some electronic aids use phonemic alphabets. Phonemic alphabet systems attempt to provide a 1:1 correspondence between the letters of the alphabet and the sounds of English, so that the pronunciation of a word can be determined from its written form. This is a problem especially in English, where a 1:1 correspondence often does not exist between the letters of the alphabet and their pronunciation in words. For example, the *O-U-G-H* combination is pronounced one way in the word *tough*, another way in the word *though*, and still another in the word *thought*. Using a phonemic alphabet, these words would be spelled differently to represent their different pronunciations.[1]

The International Phonetic Alphabet (IPA) is a phonemic alphabet used to note pronunciation for such purposes as an actor learning a dialect for a specific role, a speech pathologist taking a speech sample of a client with an articulation disorder, or a foreign speaker trying to remember the correct pronunciation of certain English words. Though most of the letters have a logical resemblance to those of the Roman alphabet, some do not. For example, the phonemes *wəz* are used to represent the word *was*.

Another example of a phonetic alphabet is SPEEC, a system that provides a 1:1 correspondence between printed and spoken words using consistent simplified orthography.[7] For example, the vowel sound in the word *was* is represented by *uh*, instead of the symbol used with the IPA. In addition to a set of single phonemes, the entries for SPEEC consist of phoneme sequences that have a high frequency of occurrence in English. For example, a SPEEC board would have *wuhz* as a selection in addition to the single phonemes making up the sequence.

An example of an electronic aid using a phonetic alphabet is the Vois (Fig. 14-8). As each letter is selected from the phonemic alphabet, the individual hears the sound it corresponds to produced by the synthesizer. In a sense, the user is sounding out a word.

Because of the correspondence between the written and spoken word, a phonemic alphabet may be easier for a speech-impaired individual to learn. The use of a phonemic alphabet with speech output may give those who are unable to spell the ability to produce open vocabularies. This was discussed further in Chapter 8 on speech output.

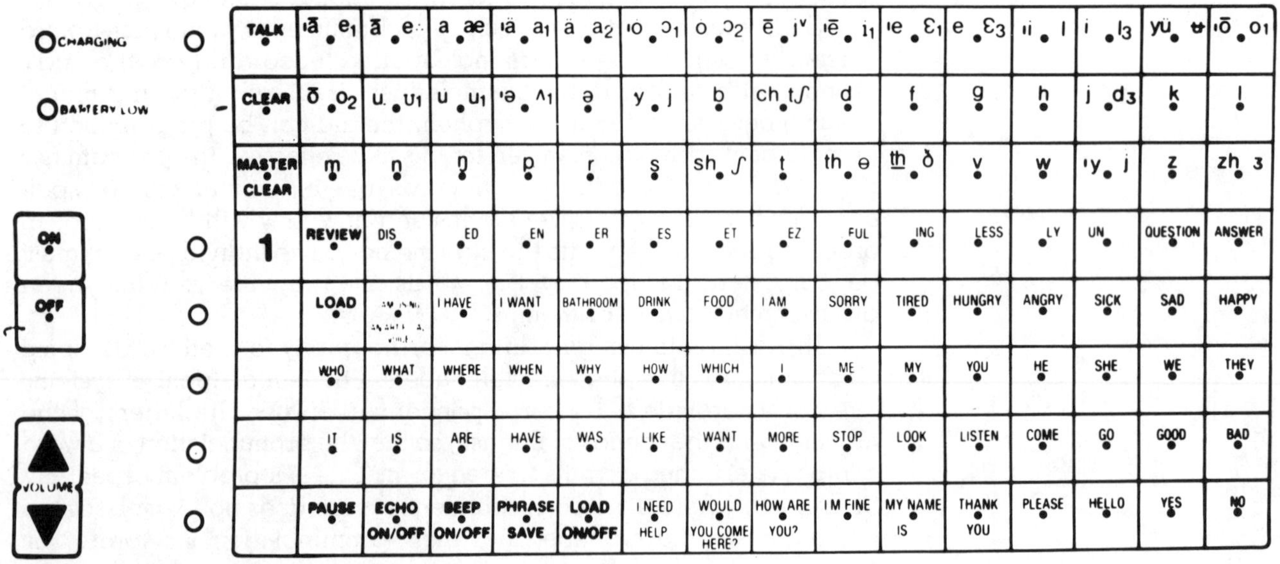

FIGURE 14-8. A phonemic alphabet (top three lines of the display) is used with the Vois 135 to create vocabulary items. (Photo by Corbit's Studio.)

REFERENCES

1. Musselwhite, C. R. & St. Louis, K. W. (1982). *Communication programming for the severely handicapped: Vocal and non-vocal strategies* (pp. 146–199). San Diego, CA: College-Hill Press.
2. Vanderheiden, G. & Lloyd, L. (in press). Communication systems and their components. In S. W. Blackstone (Ed.), *Augmentative communication: an introduction*. Rockvile, MD: American Speech and Hearing Association.
3. Silverman, F. H. (1980). *Communication for the speechless* (pp.86–87). Englewood Cliffs, NJ: Prentice-Hall.
4. Carlson, F. (1985). *Picsyms categorical dictionary*. Lawrence, KS: Baggeboda Press
5. Vanderheiden, G. (1983). Non:conversational communication technology needs of individuals with handicaps. *Rehabilitation World*, *7*, 8–9.
6. Goodenough-Trepagnier, C., Tarry, E., & Prather, P. (1982). Derivation of an efficient nonvocal communication system. *Human Factors*, *24*(2), 163–172.
7. Goodenough-Trepagnier, C. & Prather, P. (1981). Communication systems for the nonvocal based on frequent phoneme sequences. *Journal of Speech and Hearing Research*, *24*, 322–329.

15

The Vocabulary Capabilities of Communication Aids and How to Use Them

THE OPEN AND FIXED VOCABULARIES OF COMMUNICATION AIDS

The vocabulary capability of a communication aid can be open or fixed. An aid with an open vocabulary has empty, or open, space in which items can be displayed or stored and modified as needed, allowing vocabulary items to be selected and modified to meet the individual's communication needs. The items of an aid with a fixed vocabulary cannot be changed.

A nonelectronic aid or an electronic aid that visually selects items has an open vocabulary: any vocabulary item represented by any symbol can be placed on an aid's selection display by drawing or writing it. Items can be added or modified by leaving blank space on the display or by replacing old items with new ones. The number of items is limited by the space on the display unless an encoding technique is used. In most cases, items must be placed on the display by an able-bodied person because the individual usually will not have the physical ability to do this.

Some electronic aids have been preprogrammed by the manufacturer with a fixed vocabulary that cannot be changed. Few aids are manufactured with a fixed vocabulary alone because of the restrictions placed upon the items available to the individual.

The Vocaid, a portable aid producing speech output (Fig. 15-1), is an example of an aid with only a fixed vocabulary. This aid is capable of producing 36 words and phrases on each of three overlays; when the user presses a particular square, a word or phrase is spoken. The items on each overlay are related to a different situation; e.g., medical assistance, telephone calls, and game playing. These items cannot be changed for a particular user except by the manufacturer. The Vocaid also has one overlay with letters of the alphabet and numbers. The aid is capable of saying each of the letters out loud but cannot combine them to say a whole word.

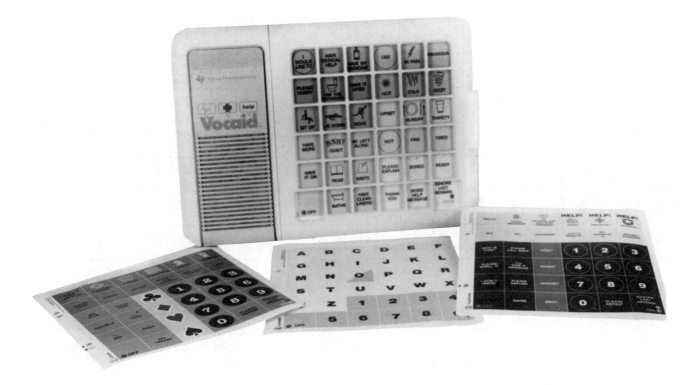

FIGURE 15-1. The Vocaid with fixed vocabulary displays. (Photo by Corbit's Studio, Bridgeport, CT.)

Many electronic aids with open vocabularies are programmable, allowing the individual using the aid or another person to create vocabulary items, store them in the aid's memory, and modify them as needed. When the target area or areas in which the item is stored is selected by the individual, it is spoken by a speech synthesizer, produced on a visual display, and/or printed on paper, depending on the output of the aid.

Most programmable electronic aids also have fixed vocabularies. The fixed items usually consist of the alphabet, word prefixes and suffixes, numbers, punctuations, and frequently used words and phrases, all of which are used to create items to be programmed into the aid and stored in its memory.

The principle advantage of a programmable electronic aid is that it allows vocabulary items to be chosen for a particular user. As a result, the individual has more useable vocabulary items and so the aid has an effectively larger vocabulary than one with only a fixed vocabulary. In addition, such an aid can be programmed with those items more frequently used by the individual, making it more effective from the standpoint of decreasing overall communication rate.[1]

An example of an aid with both fixed and open vocabularies is the Vois 135, a portable electronic aid producing speech output. The fixed vocabulary of the aid (Fig. 15-2) consists of 46 words, 10 phrases,

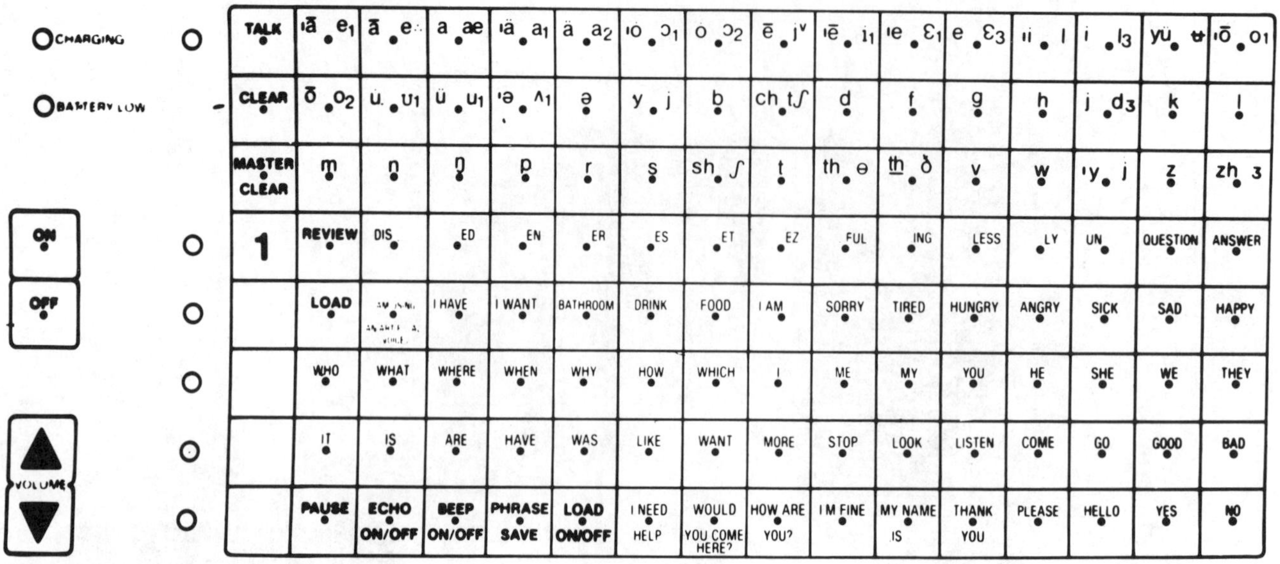

FIGURE 15-2. The fixed vocabulary of the Vois 135. (Photo by Corbit's Studio.)

12 morphemes, and 45 phonemes, which can be combined to create vocabulary items. The open vocabulary consists of four levels with 118 locations per level, which can be programmed with a total capacity of 5000 entries or units of information.

YOU NEED NOT BE A COMMPUTER PROGRAMMER TO PROGRAM AN ELECTRONIC AID

All programmable aids have a set of procedures that allow vocabulary items to be stored. Even though this section is called *programming an aid*, it is not necessary to be a computer programmer to do it. It is necessary, however, to learn how to store items in a specific location within the aid's memory. Each aid differs in the procedures that must be followed.

The programming procedures usually consist of a series of instructions that include assigning a code to an item and then storing the item in the aid's memory, usually by spelling it.

For example, in order to program the sentence *I want a cup of coffee* into SpeechPAC, an electronic aid that uses Logical Letter Coding to store items, a logical letter code would first be chosen; e.g., *W-C-C*. The programmer would then do the following:

1. Press the period key on the aid's selection display (in this case, the computer keyboard). The screen now asks, *ABBRE-VIATION=*
2. Type *WCC* and press TALK on the aid's keyboard. The visual display now asks, *PHRASE=*
3. Type *I want a cup of coffee*
4. Press TALK. SpeechPAC will speak the sentence and the screen will ask, *SOUND O/K, Y/N?*
5. *Press Y* (for yes) and the screen will go blank and the sentence will be stored in memory. (If the answer is no, there is another set of procedures to follow).)

Other programmable electronic aids have similar procedures that are as easy to follow.

Programmable aids usually allow the user to program in items independently. Even though it may be physically possible, some individuals may not have the cognitive and linguistic abilities required. In order to program an aid, an individual must first be capable of using the symbol system required to place items into the aid's memory. This usually calls for spelling, which may have to be modified if a speech synthesizer is used in order for the item to be pronounced correctly. Other aids use phonemes to create new words rather than letters of the alphabet, which may or may not be more difficult to learn than spelling. The individual must then be able to follow whatever procedures are necessary to program in items, requiring some ability to remember and follow directions. If scanning rather than direct selection is used to control the aid, this will add steps to the task of programming.

Thus, many electronic aid users do not actually program in their own vocabulary items. Rather, persons working with or assisting them may do the actual programming of items, while the user participates in selecting them.

SELECTING VOCABULARY ITEMS AND STRATEGIES

The major types of vocabulary items an individual generally needs to be able to communicate through an aid or through other modes are as follows:

- *Names of familiar partners* and others with whom he or she interacts

- *Social greetings and courtesies* (hello, how are you, fine, OK, please, thank you, you're welcome)

- *Medical and physical needs* (help, I'm in pain) *and emotional needs* (I'm bored, curses)

- *Functional vocabulary*

  This includes people, objects, locations, attributes, actions, events, and other categories the individual wants to talk about. It can also include items for specific events and activities. It is important that nonspellers have a great number of these items because they cannot produce the items themselves.

- *Clueing strategies*

  These are strategies for the individual to indicate that a needed word is not on the board and to give clues to the partner. For example, the individual could first indicate "The word is not on the board" then "I will give you clues." He could then go on to indicate, for example, "blue man car" to indicate a traffic policeman.[2]

- *Topic strategies*

    For an individual who cannot spell, these will help clarify the topic. For example, if a young child in school first indicates the topic "weekend," then the partner will know that she will refer to things that happened to her on the weekend and not at school.

- *Regulators and repair strategies*

    For both spellers and nonspellers, it is important to be able to indicate when the partner has understood or misunderstood a message, when a new item is being selected, when the individual is going to repeat an item, etc. For example, the word *space* used after a letter or word can indicate that the individual is going to select a new letter or word.

- *Conversational controllers*

    These words and phrases assist the individual in maintaining conversational control, including obtaining and maintaining speaking turns, initiating topics, interrupting a partner's turn, and changing roles from responder to initiator.[3]

    In many cases, having vocabulary items that enable the individual to maintain conversational control is more important than having specific functional vocabulary items. Such words and phrases can include initiating topics (e.g., Guess what happened to me? I need to speak with you); maintaining topics (e.g., Tell me more, Then what happened? I'm not finished yet); holding attention (e.g., Wait! Listen! Shut up!); gaining attention (e.g., Hi! Excuse me); and asking for clarification (e.g., Could you repeat that? I don't understand. What do you mean?).

- *Items to increase communication rate*

    Because able-bodied persons can converse so rapidly, the more rapidly the speech-impaired individual can produce messages, the better he or she can maintain a partner's attention and share in control of the conversation. One technique of increasing rate is by decreasing the number of movements the individual is required to make to indicate a message. For individuals who can spell, this can be done by providing whole words and phrases along with the alphabet (see the section in Chapter 14 on traditional orthography for further discussion).

    For individuals using pictographic systems, commmunication rate can be increased by placing several symbols in one target area to represent a phrase. For example, instead of having three separate symbols to express the item *I love you*, one target area can contain all three symbols or one symbol can be used to represent the entire phrase. In either case, the

FIGURE 15-3. A selection display using pictographs to represent phrases. (Photo by Corbit's Studio. The Blissymbols appearing in the photograph have been hand-drawn and are not to be considered for useage beyond this customized display. For standard Blissymbols, see *Blissymbols For Use* [Hehner, 1980].)

number of movements needed to indicate this message is decreased from three to one. Figure 15-3 demonstrates the use of one or two pictographs to represent phrases. For example, the phrase *Look in my bag*, is represented by an arrow pointing from a pair of eyeglasses into a bag.

Communication rate can be increased only when those particular items the individual communicates frequently are selected. If rarely used items are chosen, the individual's average conversation rate will not be increased significantly. For example, the phrase *I don't understand* may be used quite frequently by a particular individual, while the phrase *Today is Monday* may be used infrequently.

HOW ITEMS CAN SERVE MULTIPLE FUNCTIONS

Very often, items serve more than one function. For example, one cerebral-palsied speech-impaired adult who could not spell had an electronic aid that produced speech output. He attended a day treatment program where part of each day he and his classmates sold snacks to the staff (it was called the *Snak Shak*). By observing him during this activity, the following list of items, which would be of use to him in this situation, was gathered:

Welcome to Snak Shak
What would you like?
Donuts cost 15 cents
Coffee costs 10 cents
Here is your change
Come again!

The items were then programmed into the aid and used during Snak Shak. These items served several purposes. They were functional items that the user needed in a particular situation; they were frequently used; and they provided him with a greater degree of conversational control.

EXAMPLE: AN AID WITH MANY ITEMS SERVING DIFFERENT FUNCTIONS

Figure 15-4 shows a communication aid with many items, each serving different functions. In addition to the alphabet and numbers, there are items to assist in conversational control, such as *You didn't understand me*, *I'm thinking*, and *Slow down*; and items to help the individual communicate rapidly while playing games, such as *It's your turn*. The individual using this aid wears bilateral hearing aids, so there are items to help him to maintain the hearing aids, such as *Put it in*, *Take it out*, *Turn it off*, *Turn it on*, *There's something wrong*, and *Check the batteries*.

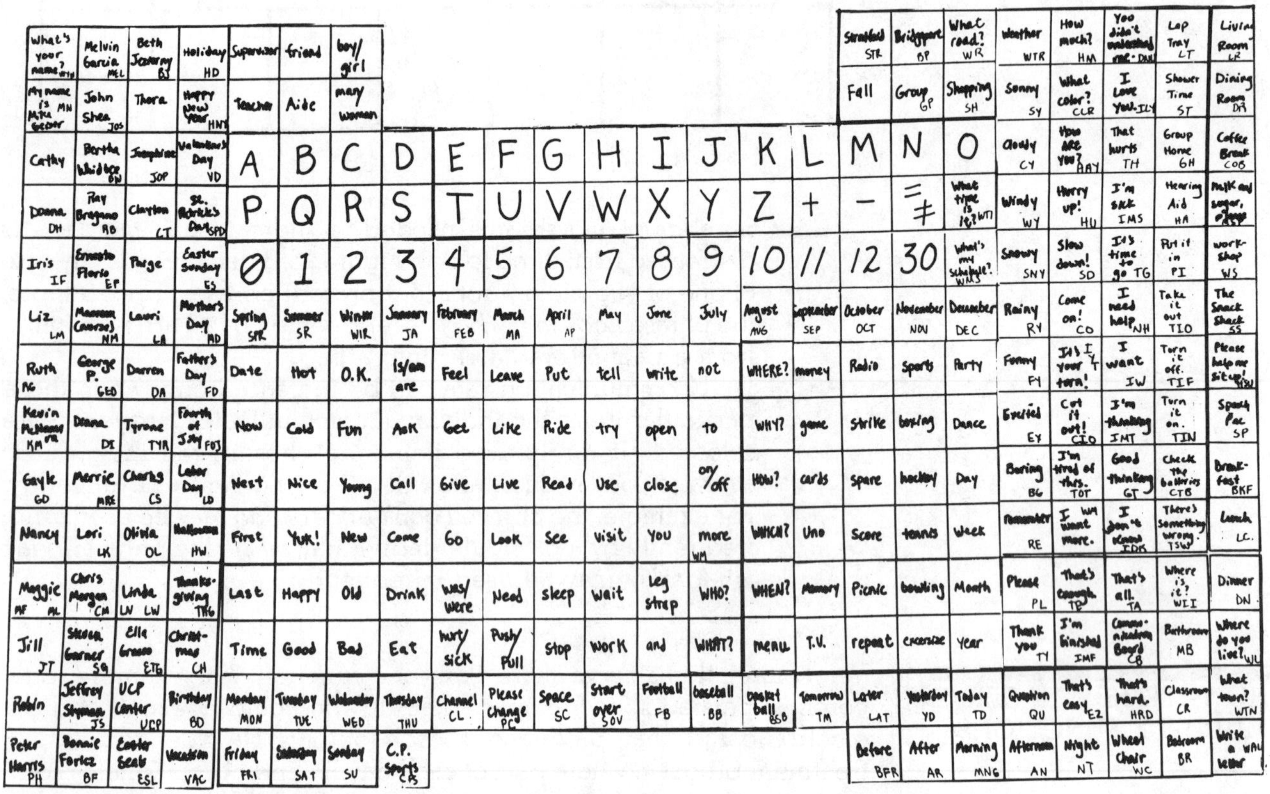

FIGURE 15-4. A selection display with many items, each serving different functions. (Photo by Corbit's Studio.)

PRACTICAL CONSIDERATIONS IN SELECTING VOCABULARY ITEMS

It is important to determine whether those items the individual can already communicate through other techniques should be included with a communication aid.

In general, if an individual uses an aid with vocabulary items that familiar partners already understand through other techniques, they will not regard the aid—nor any technique or aid introduced in the future—with much importance. For example, single nouns like food, drink, or clothing, which are included as items, may not be necessary because they are adequately taken care of by those who are familiar with the individual.

One reason to include such items, however, would be that if the individual is using an electronic aid, the item will be more effective when produced through the aid's output. For example, if the aid produces speech output, phrases like "Shut up!" or "Come here!" might be included even though the individual can communicate this through vocalization or gesture.

Another reason to include an item that is adequately communicated through other modes might be that only a limited number of familiar people can understand the individual's means of communicating it. Thus, the item is needed when the individual communicates with a stranger.

Another consideration is to select items of interest to the individual. Although selected items may be of concern to their partners, many of them may have no interest to the individual who must use them. For example, the teacher of a young child may be very concerned that the child communicate the need to go to the bathroom. The child, on the other hand, may be totally uninterested in this activity and never use this word. Meanwhile, vocabulary is omitted that communicates what the child is really interested in (phrases such as *I want to do it*, *Let me see*, *Come here*, *Get lost!*, *Bug off!* or names of classmates and other partners.

In addition, professionals often voice concern over whether to provide single words or phrases with a communication aid. The advantage of a phrase is that rate of commmunication is increased over pointing to each individual item comprising the message. The meaning of a phrase, however, usually becomes specific to a particular context or situation, reducing the openness of the vocabulary available to the individual. In contrast, a single word can represent many different meanings, depending on the context in which it is used.

For example, the phrase *Change my bib* was programmed into the electronic aid of an 8-year-old speech-impaired child because she asked that her bib be changed quite often. However, she would also select this message when she wanted to communicate *Fix my bib*, *Get my bib*, *Take off my bib* and any other message concerning the bib, because she did not have the words she needed on her board. Upon observing this, these new phrases were also programmed into the aid. In addition, she was given the single word *bib* in case she wanted to communicate some other message concerning bib that had not been programmed; e.g., *Mary's bib is pretty*. Both the single word and phrases containing the word were needed.

Another concern in providing prestored phrases is whether this could be harmful to young severely speech-impaired children, who are just developing expressive language. When a phrase is provided, the child does not have to know how to produce it because all that is needed is to select the target area containing the message. As a result, some professionals may fear that the child will never learn how to produce longer messages or develop syntactical and grammatical skills. To avoid this, they may only provide a single word in each target area so that the child will learn to formulate sentences independently.

While this concern is valid, a compromise must be made between the need for increased communication rate and the need to develop grammmar and syntax. Training should include ways to produce messages rapidly for effective conversation and ways to formulate longer, grammatically and syntactically correct messages, so that the child will know how to use them to clarify meaning and to participate in written academic activities.

REFERENCES

1. Vanderheiden, G. (1986). Personal communication.
2. Vanderheiden, G. and Lloyd, L. (in press). Communication systems and their components. In S. W. Blackstone (Ed.), *Augmentative Communication: An Introduction*. Rockville, MD: American Speech and Hearing Association.
3. Farrier, L. D., Yorkston, K. M., Marriner; N. A., & Beukelman, D. R. (1985). Conversational control in nonimpaired speakers using an augmentative communication system. *Augmentative and Alternative Communication, 1*(2), 65.

PART VI

Portability and Mounting

DIMENSIONS FOR EVALUATING PORTABILITY AND MOUNTING

Portability refers to the ability of an aid to be transported from place to place. This is determined by its size, shape, weight, and in the case of an electronic aid, its source of power. In addition, the mounting of an aid also determines its ablty to be transported as well as controlled by the individual. *Mounting* refers to positioning an aid or control switch and attaching it to a foundation in some manner.

Without sufficient portability to meet a particular communication need, an aid will not be used. Even if sufficiently portable, however, improper mounting or lack of mounting also can limit the use of an aid.

Portability and mounting can be evaluated along three dimensions: accessibility, the ability to have the aid available for a particular need; independence, the ability to use the aid without an assistant; and flexibility, the ability of the aid to be mounted and unmounted, to be transported, and to fit into the space available for it.

Nonelectronic aids can be designed with the degree of portability an individual requires, while the portability of electronic aids is fixed by the manufacturer. Both types of aids may need to be mounted for independent use and transportation.

16

How Communication Needs and Mobility Determine Portability

CATEGORIES OF PORTABILITY

When selecting electronic aids or designing a nonelectronic aid, one of the first concerns must be the degree of portability the aid must have. An aid must have the degree of portability required to meet the user's particular communication needs. These are three categories of portability:[1] stationary, desk-top, and highly portable.

Stationary

A stationary aid must be used in one physical location because it has an external power source and must be plugged into an electric outlet. It also may be too large or heavy to be carried or mounted to a wheelchair. Figure 16-1 shows the Words + Living Center, a stationary aid.

FIGURE 16-1. The Words + Living Center, an example of a stationary aid. (Photo courtesy of Words + , Inc., Sunnyvale, CA.)

Desk-Top

A desk-top aid can be carried on the laptray of a wheelchair or mounted to the chair but is too large or heavy for ambulatory use; e.g., an aid that weighs 8 pounds. Figure 16-2 shows Touch Talker, a desk-top aid.

Highly portable

A highly portable aid is small and light enough to be carried by an ambulatory or partially ambulatory individual without interfering with mobility. Figure 16-3 shows the Canon Communicator Model M, a highly portable aid.

FIGURE 16-2. Touch Talker, mounted to a wheelchair, is an example of a desk-top aid. (Photo courtesy of the Prentke Romich Company, Wooster, OH.)

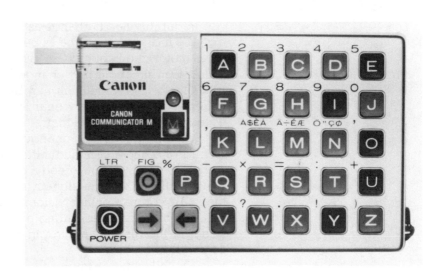

FIGURE 16-3. The Canon Communicator M, weighing 9.2 ounces, is an example of a highly portable aid. (Photo courtesy of Canon U.S.A., Inc., Lake Success, NY.)

MATCHING PORTABILITY TO NEED AND MOBILITY

The Communication Need the Aid Fulfills

The User's Mobility While Using the Aid

The portability requirements of a communication aid for a particular individual are determined by two factors: the communication need and the user's mobility.

Communication needs determine how frequently an aid must be available to the user. If an aid will be used for conversation, messaging, or writing notes in several classes, held in different locations throughout the day, then it must be accessible to the user at all times. If used only for such activities as report writing for school, it can be located in one area that the user goes to.

Mobility can be classified as ambulatory, wheelchair mobile, or nonmobile.

Ambulatory:
Independent (able to walk without assistance)
Partially ambulatory (able to walk with assistance of a walker, crutch, cane, etc.)

Wheelchair mobile:
Independent (able to move independently in a manual or motorized wheelchair)
Dependent (depends on others to propel wheelchair)
Nonmobile: Unable to sit in a wheelchair; remains in one location (e.g., bed) throughout the day.

The greater the user's mobility when using the aid, the more portable the aid must be and the more narrow are the portability choices. An ambulatory individual will need a highly portable aid, while a wheelchair mobile individual can use a highly portable or desk-top aid. A nonmobile individual can use a highly portable, desk-top, or stationary aid.

Portability needs change as mobility changes throughout the day; e.g., the individual may be in bed in the morning and evening, while in a motorized wheelchair during the greater part of the day. Unforeseen situations may change mobility; for instance, the individual with a motorized wheelchair may become more dependent if the chair's batteries have not been charged or in a place that is not easily accessible by the wheelchair.

Mobility needs also change over a period of time. For example, a child who had a communication aid placed on the lapboard of her manual wheelchair may need a different aid design when she begins to use a motorized wheelchair, so that the aid will not interfere with the chair controls or her vision. Or, an adult with ALS may initially be able to walk, necessitating a highly portable aid but, in the later stages of the disease, remain in bed most of the day and not require as portable an aid.

The following examples illustrate how communication needs and mobility of the user determine the degree of portability needed for a particular aid.

1. An individual who is able to walk with the support of a cane needs an electronic aid for face-to-face conversation and for taking notes in various classes.

Communication needs: face-to-face conversation, portable writing
Mobility status: partially ambulatory
Aid portability required: highly portable

2. As a result of a car accident, an adolescent was left quadriplegic and respirator-dependent but able to speak. He now attends high school, travelling from class to class in his motorized wheelchair. He needs an electronic aid that will allow him to do assignments and take notes in each class.

Communication need: portable writing
Mobility status: wheelchair mobile, independent
Aid portability required: desk-top or highly portable

3. An adult with ALS, who has lost the ability to speak, is respirator-dependent and remains in bed all day. She needs an electronic aid for conversation and writing notes to her attendant.

Communication needs: conversation, messaging
Mobility status: nonmobile
Aid portability required: stationary, desk top, or highly portable

CONSIDERING THE PREFERENCES OF THE USER AND CAREGIVERS

When selecting the degree of portability of an aid, the preferences of the user must be taken into account. Very often, an individual will prefer not to have a large display placed on his wheelchair, even though it does not interfere with his mobility, because he does not like the way it looks or makes him feel. An individual may not want to use an aid that blocks her ability to see other people or them from seeing her. Many users prefer than an aid be as small and unobtrusive as possible even though, because of their limited mobility, they could use a larger desk-top model that might offer them greater capabilities.

In addition to the user, the needs of those who care for the user and the aid must also be considered. An aid that must be removed each time the user is taken out of the wheelchair or that must be moved from one place to another should not be excessively heavy or cumbersome and should be easy to mount and dismount. A display that the partner must hold for the individual to see must be small and light. Since the cooperation of caregivers is crucial in determining how successfully an aid is used, their needs and preferences must be considered when selecting or designing a communication aid.

PORTABILITY MISMATCHES

A portability mismatch results from selecting an aid that is not portable enough to meet an individual's communication need. The main reason for portability mismatches is that less portable aids tend to have greater capabilities. Because providing multiple aids for different needs is expensive, the aid with the greatest capability is often purchased regardless of its portability, and then is used to meet all the individual's communication needs.

For example, an Apple IIe computer is purchased for a speech/writing-impaired cerebral-palsied child, who operates a motorized wheelchair. Although the computer has many educational and recreational applications, it can only be used in one location. This means that the child can use it at home for doing school assignments or at school for in-class work. If the child also needs an electronic aid for conversation and portable writing needs, another aid must be purchased. Attempting to use the computer as a conversation aid would be like keeping the child's mouth in a single room and requiring all speech to take place in that room.

Another example of a portability mismatch is the selection of a desk-top aid for an ambulatory individual. Because it is portable, it appears that a desk-top aid would be appropriate but, as most desk-top aids usually weigh several pounds and are larger than a three-ring notebook, they cannot easily be carried, especially by an individual who may have difficulty walking. Even if it can be carried, each time the aid is used, the individual must find a spot to rest it on.

Therefore, it is often necessary to select an aid that has the required degree of portability for some needs and not for others. When this occurs, other aids must be provided for situations where the less portable aid cannot be used. For example, where a desk-top aid producing speech output is selected for an ambulatory individual, the aid can be used for conversation needs that take place in one location; e.g., talking over the phone, conversing with a group of people sitting in one area. For conversation needs that arise while walking in the street, going shopping, or other more mobile activities, the individual will need a more portable aid.

INDIVIDUALS WHO DO NOT NEED PORTABLE AIDS

Throughout this chapter, the need for matching the portability of a conversation aid with the individual's mobility has been stressed. Since most individuals have some degree of mobility, such an aid must usually be desk-top or highly portable.

However, some severely speech-impaired individuals are nonmobile throughout the day and can be expected to remain so. These are primarily individuals with degenerative diseases, who may be difficult to position comfortably enough so that they can stay in a wheelchair or who may prefer to remain in one location. Even if this individual can be positioned well enough to sit in a wheelchair for long periods of time, if he is not independently mobile in a wheelchair, he may remain in one location most of the day.

Other individuals may be nonmobile because they are dependent on nonportable respirators. Some of these people have degenerative diseases, but they may also have suffered spinal cord injuries severe enough to affect speech or have respiratory impairments due to other conditions, such as polio.

For a nonmobile individual, a stationary aid can be used. This may be desirable because stationary aids often can fill many needs in addition to conversation (writing, drawing, calculations, environmental control, etc.), which most portable aids cannot do. Before deciding on a stationary aid, however, the individual's mobility must be carefully assessed. An individual may be remaining in bed only until he or she can be correctly positioned in a wheelchair. Individuals who depend on a respirator may be removed from the respirator on occasion or may be able to use a portable respirator. These possibilities must be checked before deciding to provide a stationary aid.

In the meantime, as technology progresses and portable aids are manufactured with the greater capabilities of stationary aids, the need to use larger aids will decrease.

REFERENCE

1. Kraat, A. W. & Sitver-Kogut, M. (1985). *Features of commercially available communication aids.* Prentke Romich Co., Phonic Ear, Don Johnston Developmental Equipment, Words Plus, Inc.

17

Mounting Communication Aids

THE NEED FOR MOUNTING AIDS AND SWITCHES

Mounting refers to the positioning of a communication aid or control switch and attaching it to a foundation in some manner. Communication aids and switches can be mounted to wheelchairs, motorized carts, laptrays, walkers, bed tables, bed rails, and many other locations, including to the user. Despite the fact that an aid is selected to meet an individual's portability requirements and that the user can select its items accurately and rapidly, an aid/switch may not be used if it is not mounted properly.

Aids and switches are mounted using a variety of hardware, some which can be bought commercially and some which must be custom designed. While some hardware is available specifically for mounting aids and switches, hardware found in camera, music, and hardware stores can also be useful. Mounting equipment also includes laptrays, which are used to position the individual as well as his communication aid.

Aids and switches may need to be mounted to make the aid accessible, for optimal control of the technique, or to enhance the user's independence.

To Achieve the Desired Degree of Aid Accessibility

If an electronic aid must be kept with the user, it must be mounted to a piece of equipment or to the user's body so that it can be transported without interfering with mobility. Without proper mounting, the individual is dependent on someone else to carry the aid. What usually happens is that even an aid that is desk-top or highly portable will be used as a stationary aid because most communication partners or caregivers will not be able to carry the aid around for the individual.

Desk-top aids and the switches used with them usually require mounting systems because they must be positioned to maximize the user's physical control and the aid's portability. Highly portable aids may be more difficult to mount if the user is ambulatory because of fewer available mounting surfaces, such as a wheelchair or laptray.

To Achieve Optimal Control of a Selection Technique

The need for proper positioning of the individual to maximize physical abilities has been previously discussed. In addition to the individual, the aid/switch must also be positioned to match the physical and visual abilities of the individual in order to gain optimal control of the selection technique used with the aid. The positon of the aid/switch includes the angle at which it must be placed and its distance from the user. It also includes how sturdy a mounting system is needed to accommodate the pressure the user will exert on it.

Mounting the aid/switch in a fixed location gives the user the consistency needed for improved control of a selection technique. If the aid/switch is in the same location each time the user activates it, it will be easier to operate than if the location constantly is changed. Correct aid/switch positioning can enhance the user's control of the aid while incorrect positioning can make it more difficult or impossible to use.

To Achieve Independent Use of the Aid

The aid/switch must be mounted so that the user is no longer dependent on a partner to hold it. If the partner must be in close physical proximity to the individual in order to control the aid, then one purpose of having an electronic aid is defeated. Additionally, the partner who holds the aid/switch influences the control over it; i.e., the partner cannot help but move the aid/switch either closer or further away as the individual activates it, so that it is difficult to know who actually is controlling the aid.

MOUNTING AN AID DURING ITS TRIAL PERIOD

It is important to mount an aid or switch during its trial period of use. While the mounting system does not need to be a permanent, it should be sufficient to allow optimal control and the required degree of portability for its intended user.

If an aid is not properly mounted during its trial period, no accurate assessment can be reached about whether it is the correct choice for the individual. For example, two desk-top electronic aids controlled through direct selection were each rented for a month for a cerebral-palsied man with a motorized wheelchair. With the first aid, no mounting system was available to position the aid properly or to allow carrying on his wheelchair. Thus, he had to use the aid only when placed flat on a table. This position interfered with his selection of target items and his ability to see the aid's selection display. In addition, he could only use the aid in one location unless someone carried it for him.

Before the second aid arrived, a mounting system was made that allowed him to carry the aid independently while he drove his motorized wheelchair. It also positioned the aid at an angle that improved both the man's physical control and his ability to see the aid's display. In this way, the individual could actually use the aid when he wanted it, enabling him to more accurately determine whether the aid met his needs.

SOURCES FOR MOUNTING SYSTEMS

Although many aids can be mounted using commercially available equipment, many others will require the services of a person who has expertise in custom-making mounting systems. In some facilities, occupational therapists have this expertise. In other facilities, a carpenter can do this or a client's relative or friend who has carpentry skills and is willing to volunteer the time. When no mounting services are available, their availability at other facilities should be investigated.

However, even in large facilities where there are many physically disabled persons, often no one is available to build mounting systems because of a lack of funds for such a person or because such a person is very difficult to find. It may also be because the need for these services was never realized.

In order to provide appropriate mounting systems, a number of different approaches must be used. Commercially available equipment is desirable because it can be obtained quickly and may be less expensive than having a system custom-made but, depending on the needs of the individual and the design of the aid, all aids and switches cannot be properly mounted with commercially available equipment.

Mounting must be customized when no commercially available item will suffice. If an in-house person does not have the expertise to make a specific item, a consultant or outside facility must be used. It is rare that one approach will provide for all mounting needs. The following approaches can be taken to obtain mounting.

Purchasing Commercially Available Equipment

Some equipment, such as laptrays upon which aids and switches can be mounted, can be bought through medical supply catalogues. Very often, other equipment not specifically made for mounting communication aids can be used for this purpose.

Companies that manufacture electronic aids also manufacture mounting systems for their switches and aids. Kits are also available that can be used for mounting any aid permanently, for evaluation purposes prior to making a permanent system, or for replacing parts as needed. The ZYGO Adaptive Fixtures Kit, shown in Figure 17-1, is such a kit.

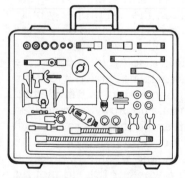

FIGURE 17-1. The ZYGO Adaptive Fixtures Kit, a commercially available mounting kit. (Drawing courtesy of ZYGO Industries, Inc., Portland, OR.)

Custom-Making Equipment

A parent, other relative, or friend of an individual often is willing to volunteer to make equipment. However, these services may no longer be available if the individual leaves the facility, and the volunteer may only want to make items for that individual.

Local groups of retired carpenters and machinists may have members willing to volunteer their services.

An individual can be brought to an evaluation center that has expertise in augmentative communication or in adaptive equipment.

A person with expertise in building adaptive equipment may be willing to come to a facility or a home and make the equipment for an individual. This is preferable to traveling to an outside center because the expert can meet all the team members working with the individual and observe the environment. The drawback to this is if something needs to be modified or fixed, the facility does not have anyone on premises who can readily do this.

Medical supply companies that sell wheelchairs and lapboards may also make mounting systems.

Although having a part- or full-time adaptive equipment person on the premises is the most desirable arrangement, it can also be the most difficult to achieve because of the need to justify the funds for a new position. Very often, it is best to try all the earlier suggestions first, as evidence is gathered to build a case to hire an on-staff person.

Usually, it is also very difficult to find someone with the expertise to build these systems. Many persons will have the experience in working with wood, for example, but not in metal or plastic, which is also desirable when making mounting systems.

Someone who is available to custom-make mountings should not be asked to make systems already available commercially and appropriate for an individual. Many commercially available items are too costly or difficult to duplicate and should usually be bought from their manufacturer. In general, the mounting technician's skills should be reserved for items that cannot be purchased commercially.

GUIDELINES FOR DESIGNING AND EVALUATING A MOUNTING SYSTEM

When a mounting system is being custom-made, the ability of clinicians to clearly communicate the type of system that an individual needs and the features the system must have is crucial. In addition, the clinician's ability to assess the effectiveness of the mounting system, whether it is custom-made or purchased commercially, is important. The following guidelines can be used in designing and assessing a mounting system for an aid or control switch:[1]

Step 1: Identify the functions and major constraints of the mounting system:

A. *What does the mounting system need to do?*
- Will the system attach the aid/switch to a stationary fixture (e.g., a table), to a moving vehicle (e.g., a wheelchair), or to some other object?
- Will the system position the aid/switch?
- How must the aid/switch be positioned? At what angle? How far from the user?

B. What physical constraints of the user need to be taken into account?

- Will the user's range of motion limit placement of the aid; e.g., will arms bang into the aid when moved, will head accidentally activate the switch?
- Will the user's positioning tend to change so that the position of the aid/switch needs to be adjustable?
- How much pressure will the user exert on the aid/switch? How sturdy must the mounting system be?

C. What environmental constraints must be taken into account?

- Will the individual use the aid/switch in a number of positions so that it must be removable; e.g., use it both in wheelchair and in bed?
- Will the individual use other aids and devices; e.g., to operate a motorized wheelchair? If so, where is the control located?
- Will the aid/switch interfere with other activities; e.g., watching television, using a computer, eating?

D. Does the mounting system need to be dismounted?

- Will the mounting system need to be removed and replaced frequently for such activities as using a toilet? If a mounting system is not easy to remount, it usually will not be remounted.
- Will unmounting the system interfere with the collapse of a wheelchair for transport? When in a car, the individual's wheelchair is often placed in the trunk. If this process involves removing an aid, a mounting system, and a seating system, collapsing a chair, etc., then the process can become quite complicated. Additionally, a system that does not easily or quickly remove from the chair makes it very difficult to put the chair in the trunk.[2]
- Will there be room to store the mounting system during transport; e.g., in a van that transports many individuals to and from home? If the mounting system is too large, the aid will only be used in one place.

Step 2: Together with the mounting technician and the individual, discuss the functions and constraints of the system including possible foundations for attaching a mounting system (e.g., wheelchair frame, lapboard); possible fixtures to connect the aid/switch to the foundation (e.g., a flexible gooseneck, a rigid metal pipe); the method of attachment (e.g., will holes need to be drilled for a screw attachment, can pressure sensitive velcro be used); the ability to quickly disconnect the mounting system; the ability to fold the system for transport in a car trunk.

Step 3: The mounting system is designed and assembled.

Step 4: The system is used in a trial period. During this period, the mounting system is evaluated while the individual uses it, taking into consideration the following:

- Does the system interfere with transfers?
- Does it interfere with mobility by blocking vision? by increasing the width of a chair so that it is more difficult to manipulate? by making the chair heavier?
- Is the system strong enough?
- Can it be easily removed or swung away?
- Can it be easily remounted?

Step 5: Modify the original mounting system, if necessary, and reevaluate it.

It is crucial that the system be continually modified until it meets the individual's needs within the physical and environmental constraints. If the user or caregivers are uncomfortable with the system, it will probably not be used.

EXAMPLE: HOW MOUNTING MADE A DIFFERENCE

Chris, a 21-year-old, severely speech-impaired individual with cerebral palsy, used a nonelectronic communication board consisting of a pictographic system whose items he indicated through the Viewpoint Optical Indicator, a light beam worn on his forehead (see Chapter 10 for a description of this aid).

In order to accurately indicate items with this aid, the selection display had to be placed at about a 45° angle in front of him. Initially, there was no way to mount the display to Chris's lapboard securely. Additionally, attaching it would have interfered with Chris's field of vision, since he could not see over or around it.

Therefore, for many months, Chris's communication aid was attached to a wooden easel. This device stood in a corner of Chris's classroom and was brought to him by his communication partner when he asked for it by looking toward it. The device was placed directly in front of Chris and was removed when he finished his conversation (Fig. 17-2).

The aid's lack of portability severely limited its use. Chris was totally dependent on his partner's cooperation to bring him the aid. If he could not turn his head toward the device or if he were not in the room with it, he could not ask for it.

Finally, through the services of an adaptive equipment consultant, a custom-made display was built for Chris (Fig. 17-3). This consisted of a display that could be folded down onto the lapboard when Chris did not need it. When he wanted to use it, a message was attached to the back of the display that asked his partner to lift it up. When the display was pulled down, the message lay flat on top of the lapboard so that Chris could indicate it with his light beam.

This mounting system allowed Chris to have his aid accessible at all times when he was in his wheelchair. He was no longer dependent on his partner to bring the aid to him, and he could take the aid with him wherever he went. Because of this, the number of people he communicated with increased. As a result, it soon became clear that Chris would also need an electronic aid to provide for his expanding communication needs.

FIGURE 17-2. A mounting system limiting the use of a communication aid to one location. (Photo by Corbit's Studio, Bridgeport, CT.)

FIGURE 17-3. A portable mounting system, allowing a communication aid to be more accessible to the user. (Photo by Corbit's Studio. Mounting system by Mark Cavanna, Cerebral Palsy Center, Bridgeport, CT.)

FIGURE 17-4. A custom-made mounting system for a communication aid designed not to interfere with the user's control of his motorized wheelchair. (Photo by Corbit's Studio. Mounting system by Independent Specialty Co., Middle Haddam, CT.)

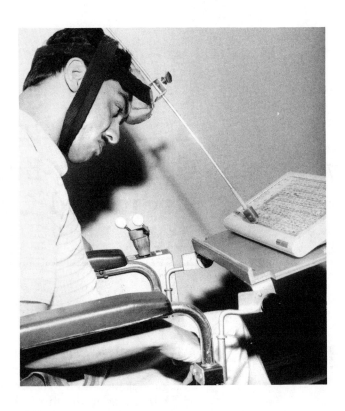

EXAMPLE: MOUNTING SYSTEM FOR AN AID

Figure 17-4 shows a custom-made mounting system for a communication aid. The system was made, rather than purchased commercially because no available system could meet the requirements of this particular individual, Melvin. As can be seen from the photo, Melvin has a motorized wheelchair, which he controls with a joystick mounted at his left hand. Thus, the first requirement was that the system not interfere with control of his chair nor his vision as he travels. The second requirement was that the system hold the aid in the best position for Melvin to directly select items from its display but that it also be adjustable at different angles for other activities. For example, Melvin paints very well with his headstick and needs a surface at a greater angle for this task. At mealtimes, Melvin needs a flatter surface on which to place his food and eating utensils. The final requirement was that the system be designed so that Melvin's knees did not continually knock into it. Because he has athetoid cerebral palsy, Melvin's knees often fly up in the air and can hit a surface with great force.

As can be seen, the system was designed to meet these requirements. It is also easily unmounted and mounted so that others can easily handle it.

REFERENCES

1. Adapted from Assistive Device Center. (1982). *A guide to controls* (p.59). Stanford, CA: Children's Hospital at Stanford.
2. Vanderheiden, G. (1986). Personal communication.

PART VII

Computer-Based and Dedicated Communication Aids

THE COMPUTER TRAP

A father calls an augmentative communication resource center to inquire about hardware and software for his 3-year-old speech-impaired son. He has just been to a conference on microcomputer applications and has not seen anything that he thinks might be appropriate. He throws in a few terms like *unicorn keyboard* and *mouse*.

When asked about how his son communicates with those around him, the father is vague and only mentions a picture book that the child uses at home to indicate things he wants. The father then becomes annoyed with this line of questioning. He is interested in computers and what they can do for his son. After all, if he gives him access to a computer, isn't that better than a homemade picture board or one of those over-priced dedicated communication aids?

This well-meaning father, along with many clinicians, speech-impaired individuals, and their families and friends has fallen into the "computer trap." This is the belief that it is more important for a speech-impaired individual to use a computer than to communicate and that computers are better than dedicated aids and somehow will compensate automatically for the communication and cognitive problems of the speech-impaired individual. These beliefs reflect a general confusion between communicating and using a computer, as if the two were interchangeable.

The computer trap is partly due to society's belief that computers are a panacea for educational, vocational, and even personal problems, a belief fostered by extensive advertising about the wonders, and even the necessity, of computers.

Additionally, the speech-impaired individual may not have been given any effective means of communication, so that family and friends may have never seen him or her successfully having a conversation. They may not understand that it is within the speech-impaired individual's ability to communicate more than yes or no. All they may have seen is their spouse or child unable to do anything independently. In comparison to doing nothing, using a computer seems like an excellent idea.

In many cases, providing a speech/writing-impaired individual with access to computers may open the way to pursuing educational and vocational goals. In fact, for disabled persons, the ability to use computers may soon become (as already has happened in many situations) a prerequisite for obtaining an education or pursuing a career. However, use of a computer to participate in these activities would not eliminate the need for an effective means of communication, but simply make providing it more important. Regardless of how well an individual uses a computer, he or she still will need a communication aid.

Another result of the computer trap is that computer-based communication aids often are considered better than dedicated aids, because consumers believe they can also perform other computer functions. It would appear that the purchaser is getting two aids—one for computing and one for conversation—for the price of one. In reality, however, a decision to purchase a computer-based or dedicated aid must be based on how well the aid matches the individual's needs and abilities.

In this last chapter, an attempt will be made to clarify the differences between computer-based and dedicated aids and to provide guidelines for selecting an aid.

18

Deciding Between a Computer-Based and a Dedicated Communication Aid

HOW A MICROCOMPUTER IS TRANSFORMED INTO A COMMUNICATION AID

A microcomputer consists of standard hardware designed for able-bodied persons. It is transformed into a conversation or writing aid through custom-written software and hardware adaptations, such as special keyboards, selection displays, speech synthesizers, etc. This is in contrast to a dedicated aid, which consists of custom-designed hardware and software to be used for communication by speech/writing-impaired individuals.

A number of communication aid packages (software and hardware adaptations) are available for several computers, each offering different vocabulary capabilities and selection techniques to the user. Of the portable computers, the Epson HX-20 is most widely used to date as a communication aid, because it has both a visual display and printer. Of the stationary computers, the greatest amount of customized hardware and software is available for the Apple II family. As technology develops, other computers can be expected to be used more frequently for communication as well.

Custom-designed software enables messages to be stored and then produced through the computer's printed or spoken outputs. These messages can be produced through the speech synthesizer or displayed on its screen and printed on its printer. Custom-designed software also enables the computer to be controlled through a technique other than directly selecting keys on a keyboard display. For example, with SCAN-TALK, a custom-written program, SpeechPAC can be controlled through scanning. Using other programs, a portable microcomputer also can be controlled through techniques such as Morse code with one or two switches or direct selection through an alternate keyboard or with a light beam. Figure 18-1 shows various selection techniques that can be used. Although this flexibility also is offered with many dedicated aids, it is easier to have multiple selection techniques with computer-based aids, since they are more easily programmed.[1]

Thus, through custom-designed software, a single computer can be transformed into many communication aids with a variety of features.

FIGURE 18-1. SpeechPAC, an example of a computer-based aid controlled by a number of selection techniques. (Photo courtesy of Adaptive Communication Systems, Inc., Pittsburgh, PA.)

THE DIFFERENCE BETWEEN A COMPUTER-BASED AND A DEDICATED COMMUNICATION AID

In the process of selecting an electronic communication aid, there is a tendency to categorize aids as either computers or dedicated aids then compare them along those lines. This is because, in the past, computers were generally stationary and very different from portable dedicated aids. However, with the current generation of computer-based aids, there often is little difference between many of them and dedicated aids.[1]

For example, for an individual who needs to use a scanning technique, there are many similarities between the features of SpeechPAC and Light Talker, a dedicated aid. Both have small visual displays and built-in speech. Both can be controlled by a variety of selection techniques, including scanning, optical headpointing, and directed scanning. Both are fully portable, battery-operated, and built into a single unit. Both can be purchased only from their manufacturers or the manufacturers' dealers. Both must be maintained by their manufacturers (a SpeechPAC cannot be taken to an Epson computer dealer for repair because there are too many custom modifications).

The Epson computers used as SpeechPACs are almost never used with any software other than a program from its manufacturer. Similarly, the Light Talker is used only with one of the several different software packages that can be secured from its manufacturer to run in the Light Talker. Essentially, a decision to purchase a SpeechPAC or a Light Talker would be based totally upon factors other than whether one uses a computer.

Thus, the selection of an aid for a particular individual should be completely independent of whether it is dedicated or computer-based. Rather, it should be based solely upon the ability of the aid to meet the individual's needs, utilizing his or her abilities and circumventing his or her constraints.[1]

In order for an aid to be considered a candidate for selection, whether it is computer-based or dedicated, its features must match the communication needs and abilities of the particular speech/writing-impaired individual. It must produce the outputs the individual requires to meet communication needs. It must have the degree of portability required, be controlled by a technique the individual can use accurately, and have vocabulary capabilities within his or her cognitive/linguistic abilities and requirements.

The extent of the evaluation required with each aid will vary depending upon the amount and type of information needed about the individual's performance with it. For example, the individual's ability to select items from the aid may already be known but his ability to use the aid's encoding system may not be. Ideally, at one point, all aids being considered should be present to compare more closely the individual's performance with each one.

If the primary features of both aids equally match the communication needs and abilities of the individual, the quality and capabilities of these features must then be compared. For each individual, one or more features will prove more important than others, which may be the deciding factor in selection.

ASPECTS OF COMMUNICATION AID FEATURES TO COMPARE

Speech as output:
- Intelligibility
- Naturalness
- Volume controlled by user

Visual display as output:
- Ease of viewing for user and partner
- Number of characters displayed at one time
- Size of characters
- Correction capabilities

Printer as output:
- Size of paper
- Type of printer
- Size of characters
- Part of aid or physically separate

Portability:
- Ease of carrying (size, shape, weight)
- Ease of mounting and unmounting

Selection technique:
- Ease of physical control
- Accuracy of control
- Complexity of operation
- Ability to use different techniques

Vocabulary capabilities:
- Ease of storing and retrieving vocabulary items
- Capability for user to program items
- Size of memory to store items

Other aspects to be considered include
- Ability of user to turn the aid on and off independently
- Ability to increase conversation rate through rate enhancement techniques
- Ability to borrow the aid for a period of time for a trial period
- Maintenance/repair record; i.e., is the aid reliable or does it require repairs often? is it durable?
- Length of time the aid has been commercially available; is this a relatively new aid or an aid that has been used by others for a period of time?
- Cost; is there a significant difference between the cost of the aids?
- Continuing availability; is there a likelihood that the aid will be discontinued in the near future? will a new model with greater capabilities be introduced in the near future? in that case, will the manufacturer upgrade the model being presently purchased?

Computers tend to be somewhat stronger in some of these areas, while dedicated aids tend to be stronger in others. However, both computer-based and dedicated aids continuing to evolve and improve, and as they do so, they have more and more of each other's positive attributes. The result is that it is no longer easy to categorize attributes of aids by method of construction so that each aid must be evaluated individually.[1]

USING A DEDICATED OR COMPUTER-BASED COMMUNICATION AID TO PROVIDE COMPUTER ACCESS

Another aid feature to consider in selecting among communication aids is whether a particular aid can provide the individual access to another computer used to perform other functions. In general, the types of computers that provide such access are stationary computers that can run a variety of software programs. Providing access to these computers can be considered a communication need because it presents a similar problem; i.e., both involve the transfer of information that could be handled through a special keyboard or interface of some sort. Moreover, the techniques, interfaces, and aids necessary to provide these transfers are extremely similar, if not identical.[2]

For example, a situation in which this need occurred is the case of Carly, a 6-year-old, speech/writing-impaired child, who attends a mainstreamed class. There is a computer in the classroom that all her able-boldied classmates use with various educational programs designed to help them learn to spell and read. One program is Stickybear® ABC, a program that requires a child to activate a letter key on the keyboard for a cartoon representing a word beginning with that letter to appear on the video monitor.

Carly is unable to use direct selection and so cannot operate the keyboard the way the rest of her classmates do. Rewriting the program for her so that she can use it would be extremely expensive and only give her access to that one program.

Other techniques have been developed that are less expensive and can give individuals such as Carly the ability to use any program able-bodied persons can use. These techniques allow a computer to be operated through whatever selection technique the physically disabled person is able to use, while the computer reacts as if the person were using its keyboard. Because the computer cannot tell that the keyboard is not being used, the technique is referred to as *transparent*.[3]

One type of transparent technique, called a *keyboard emulating interface,* allows an electronic communication aid, either dedicated or computer based, to act as the computer's keyboard. The keyboard emulating interface consists of a module inserted between the computer's keyboard and the main computer circuit board. The aid used to control the computer is connected to the emulator. The output of the aid is fed into the keyboard emulating interface, which then feeds it into the computer as if it had been typed on the keyboard. To the computer, the emulating interface looks electrically identical to the keyboard. Therefore, it cannot tell whether signals are coming from the computer's keyboard or the communication aid, and so reacts the same.[3]

With a keyboard emulating interface, the child described earlier can use her row-column scanning electronic communication aid as the computer keyboard (Fig. 18-2). In the case of Stickybear® ABC, when she selects a desired letter on the communication aid's selection display, the cartoon for that letter will appear on the computer's video monitor, just as it would if she had pressed a key on the keyboard.

In order for an electronic communication aid to be used with the standard keyboard emulating interface, it must have an RS232 connector. While all computer-based aids have this connector, not all dedicated aids do. Thus, in selecting an electronic aid, an RS232 connector may be desirable, if the user is also interested in having access to other computers.

FIGURE 18-2. Use of an electronic aid to provide access to a computer. (Drawing by Ava Barber, New York, NY.)

COMPARING THE COST OF COMPUTER-BASED AND DEDICATED AIDS

Because of the hesitancy of third-party payers to fund communication aids, the cost of an aid is often a major concern. In general, computers are believed to cost less than dedicated aids. As a result, computers, rather than dedicated aids, are often prescribed for speech/writing-imapaired individuals on the basis of cost alone. This has frequently resulted in selection of an inappropriate aid.

A main reason that the microcomputer began to be used as a communication aid was that it could provide the same functions as a dedicated aid at a lower cost. This is because the microcomputer consists of standard hardware designed to be used for a variety of purposes by the general population. It is lower in price than a dedicated aid because it is produced in greater volume. Dedicated aids consist of special hardware systems using custom-designed software. Because they are produced for a limited group of consumers, they are produced in low volume, which is inherently more costly. As a result, dedicated aids are more expensive than computers.

Although it is true that a computer itself costs less than a dedicated aid, because custom-designed software and hardware adaptations are required to transform it into a communication aid, the cost of the portable computer begins to approach that of comparable dedicated aids. For example, at this writing, an Epson HX-20 computer costs about $800 while the same computer transformed into a communication aid costs about $2200. At the same time, the cost of dedicated aids has decreased. A comparable dedicated aid can cost from $2500 to $4000.

The cost of any aid decreases if it can be used over a longer period of time. Any aid that can continue to be used as the individual's needs or abilities change will be less expensive than one that cannot be adapted to change.

Thus, although the initial cost of a dedicated aid and a computer are similar, the final cost is determined by how well each aid meets all the individual's communication needs and abilities over time.

EXAMPLE:SELECTING AMONG SEVERAL COMMUNICATION AIDS

Tim is a 25-year-old man who, at the age of 16, suffered a traumatic brain injury from a car accident. He is now severely speech-impaired and walks with the use of a cane. Tim communicates through finger spelling and gesturing. He is able to write, although he does so very slowly and laboriously. In addition, he uses a portable communication aid that produces speech output, which he purchased soon after the accident. This aid is used to communicate with those who do not understand finger spelling and for communication over the phone or in groups. Tim is able to carry the aid, which weighs $5\frac{1}{2}$ pounds, on a shoulder strap.

Tim has used his electronic aid for five years and would now like to purchase a new aid. He knows that, since the time he purchased it, many new aids have been developed with greater capabilities, of which he would like to take advantage.

Tim's communication needs have also changed. After living at home with his parents for several years, he has just entered college and is taking two courses. During the school year, he lives on campus and, during vacation, stays with his family, who live nearby. In order to travel, Tim frequently takes cabs by himself. Thus, his need to communicate with strangers has increased.

In addition to conversation, Tim now also has writing needs: writing reports, taking notes and exams in class, etc. He is able to write legibly but it is slow and fatiguing and he is unable to do assignments as quickly as his classmates. He has an electric typewriter at home but he cannot use it with speed and the quality of work he produces is poor because he makes many errors that he cannot correct independently. At this point, a portable aid with a visual display and printer would be very useful to him.

Despite his need for writing, Tim's first choice of communication aid is the newest model of his current aid, which also produces only speech output and has been available for about a year. He has rented it for a month, became very familiar with its operation and capabilities, and is able to use it accurately. This aid is much lighter than his current aid (it weighs only $2\frac{1}{2}$ pounds) and has greater memory capacity. Tim can trade in his old aid and purchase the new aid at a reduced price.

However, considering Tim's need for a display and printer, two other aids are considered. One is a portable computer-based aid that produces speech and printed output. The other is a portable dedicated aid with a visual display. A printer can be bought separately and attached to the aid when needed.

Tim is able to operate all three aids equally well: he can physically control them, store and retrieve vocabulary items using their programming procedures, and use their encoding techniques. Because he is more familiar with the programming procedures and the method of creating vocabulary items with the newer model of his current aid, he is faster using it but would be able to increase his rate with the other two after some practice.

Tim feels that his most important need, however, is to have a portable conversation aid. Thus, the most important features to him are portability and speech intelligibility, while the visual display and printer are a secondary concern. The following features of the three aids are compared.

Portability

The portable computer weighed 5 pounds and measured $8\frac{1}{2} \times 14\frac{1}{2}''$ $\times 1\frac{3}{4}$ inches. The dedicated aid with visual display weighed approximately 5 pounds and measured $13 \times 8\frac{7}{8} \times 2\frac{3}{4}$ inches. The speech-output-only aid weighed $2\frac{1}{2}$ pounds and measured $8\frac{1}{2} \times 8\frac{1}{2}$ inches. The extra size and weight of the computer and the visual-display–dedicated aid made either one more cumbersome for Tim to carry.

Intelligibility and Quality of Speech

All three aids were brought into the same room. Tim produced the same messages with each of them. The intelligibility and quality of the speech-output-only aid was superior to the other two aids to strangers who had never heard the output of any of the devices, as well as to Tim and others who were familiar with Tim's old aid.

The possibility of increasing the intelligibility of the speech produced by the other aids was not fully explored because Tim felt that their larger size and weight had eliminated them as possibilities.

Based on Tim's two most important concerns, portability and speech intelligibility, his final decision was to purchase the new speech-output-only aid. To meet his need for a visual display and printer, Tim also purchased a highly portable aid with a wide-column printer and single-line visual display, which he carries in his knapsack. He often uses it for face-to-face conversation with a familiar partner and for some writing needs in class, although it has limited editing capabilities and a small printer. His future plan is to purchase a stationary computer with word processing capabilities, a full-page printer, and a video monitor. The computer can also be used for other functions, such as to run educational programs to supplement his classwork and for recreation.

Tim's story is an example of how a choice between communication aids can be made and how a final decision must be based on the needs and preferences of the user.

THE CONTINUING AVAILABILITY OF COMPUTER-BASED AND DEDICATED AIDS

In considering a computer as a communication aid, the continued availability of a particular model may be of greater concern to some people than that of a particular dedicated aid. This is understandable because new computers appear and disappear on a weekly basis. Many professionals in the health and education professions bought Apple II Pluses, only to have them quickly replaced by IIes and IIcs, which are not compatible with much of the II Plus software. There is panic at the thought that as soon as the speech/writing-impaired individual receives a new computer-based aid, the manufacturer will decide to stop producing it.

In general, the microcomputer industry is, and will continue to be, highly competitive. Decisions whether to continue to manufacture a specific computer will be based on availability of newer, cheaper technologies that rapidly replace older model computers.[1]

Of particular concern to communication aid users are the future of portable computers. It is possible that a particular portable computer used as a communication aid could be discontinued. However, if such a thing occurred, the effect may not be as devastating as it initially would appear.

For example, if Epson stopped producing the HX-20, for which several communication aid packages have been designed, the speech-impaired individual could still use it as a communication aid as long as it met his or her needs and operated well. The manufacturer of the communication software and hardware adaptations would still be responsible for maintaining and modifying those adaptations. The software manufacturer could even buy a supply of the computers so that, if no longer manufactured, there would still be enough of them to sell for a period of time after the computer went out of production.

This situation has already occurred, not with a computer but with a portable calculator originally designed to be used by able-bodied persons, which could also be used as an aid with a visual display and a printer by those individuals with good direct-selection ability. When the company stopped manufacturing this device, several communication aid vendors and manufacturers managed to buy the remaining aids so that they would still be available to speech-impaired individuals. At this writing, the aid is still in demand and a limited supply is still available through selected dealers.

As with computers, decisions whether to continue production of dedicated aids are based on the availability of new, less expensive technologies that manufacturers want to incorporate into their products. In fact, over the last few years, production of many dedicated aids has been stopped while more and more new aids have been introduced.

For example, the Prentke Romich Company has manufactured a series of aids, each of which have been an improvement over the prior aid in design and capabilities, as well as lower in cost. These are the Express 1, Express 3, Touch Talker, and Light Talker. The same is true for Phonic Ear, which first produced the Handivoices 110 and 120 and now produces Vois 130, 135, and 140. Although each aid represented an improvement over the prior model, many individuals were left with aids bought only a year or so earlier but no longer being manufactured. Thus, dedicated aids are not immune from discontinuation. However, most manufacturers offer trade-in policies on discontinued models, so that the individual can pay less for a newer model.

It also is often to the manufacturer's advantage to offer new aids to those using older models, so that they do not have to maintain and repair them. Like parts for old cars, refrigerators, or any machine, parts for aids no longer being manufactured soon become unavailable and personnel are no longer trained in repairing them. Discontinued aids soon become an unwelcome problem, for both the manufacturer and the user.

Technology is changing rapidly for both computers and dedicated aids, and both types of aids can be expected to be replaced with greater frequency than previously. As technology for dedicated aids and computers advances, many individuals will want to take advantage of these developments as their systems wear out or as new aids become available that meet their needs much more effectively.[1]

WAITING FOR THE FUTURE

Future developments in technology will result in electronic communication aids that will be more portable, cost less, have larger memories, have more intelligible speech output, have the ability to perform multiple functions, and have many other improved capabilities. Because technology is changing so rapidly, the question frequently arises as to whether it is better to postpone purchase of an electronic communication aid until a "better" aid is developed.

For example, the parents of a speech/writing-impaired child were disappointed with the quality of speech output available with the electronic aids that had been rented for her for a trial period of use. They wanted to postpone purchase of an aid until more intelligible and natural sounding speech output were available.

In another example, a 35-year-old woman, who has muscular dystrophy and is respirator-dependent, lived at home with her parents. She wanted an aid that would allow her to carry on conversations with her nurses and parents more rapidly than she could through them reading her lips. Because of her severely limited physical abilities, she had to use row-column scanning or Morse code as a selection technique. She considered these to be too slow and wanted to wait for an aid that produced messages more rapidly.

In each instance, a decision to postpone purchase must be made in relation to the individual's needs, the specific situation, and other communication modes available. In the case of the speech-impaired child mentioned above, the main purpose of an electronic aid is to allow her to do independent written work and to provide her with feedback, by allowing her to view her messages on a visual display. The speech output will enable the child to communicate with her peers in school but is not needed for face-to-face conversation because she has a nonelectronic aid that she uses effectively. Although speech output is important, it is secondary to the need for a visual display and printer. Thus, a decision to delay purchase of an aid would only further delay the child's academic and communication growth and development.

If the child's needs were different, if speech output were the most important need, a decision to postpone purchase would have to be based on whether an accurate assessment of the speech intelligibility of available aids had been made. If it were totally accurate and all aids were considered unintelligible, then a postponement might be wise. If an aid could be found that was somewhat intelligible after partner training, then the negative effects upon the child of delaying purchase would have to be weighed relative to the need for highly intelligible speech. For example, would the lack of peer interaction seriously affect the child's social development? Would it prevent the child from participating in activities with other children?

In addition, the likelihood must be investigated that an aid will be available with the capabilities or qualities the individual wants within a time period he or she is able or willing to wait. For example, will a new, more intelligible speech output aid be available in the near future? Frequently, when a new aid will be available that appears to meet the needs of an individual, vendors who are knowledgeable about new developments will tell the consumer to help make a decision about whether to postpone purchase. This information can also be found out from a variety of publications.

The reality of the individual's expectations must also be examined. In the case of the woman with muscular dystrophy, an aid that could significantly increase her rate of communication will probably not be available in the near future. For the most part, communication rates can be expected to remain in their present range, especially for someone who cannot use direct selection. In addition, the woman has a degenerative condition. This alone would indicate the need for an electronic aid *now*, not five years from now.

When no aid is expected in the immediate future that will have the capability or quality the individual wants, it is best to reevaluate what is currently available. The possibility of rental should also be explored if the individual is truly dissatisfied with what is available but needs to have certain needs met now. Compromises need to be made between what is wanted and what is available.

Thus, selecting electronic aids is an on-going process throughout the life of the speech/writing-impaired individual, who may use several different aids. Although a more intelligible and portable aid may be available in three years, an even better one probably will be available three years later. Since there will always will be new and more effective developments, care must be taken that waiting for a better aid does not mean waiting forever.

REFERENCES

1. Vanderheiden, G. (1986). Personal communication.
2. Vanderheiden, G. (1983). Nonconversational communication technology needs of individuals with handicaps. *Rehabilitation World*, 7(2), 9–10.
3. Vanderheiden, G. (1982). Computers can play a dual role for disabled individuals. *Byte, 7*(2), 146.

Subject Index

A

Abbreviation/expansion, use in encoding technique, 85
Adapted electronic aids, 6
Aided scanning technique, 3
Assessment of augmentative communication,
  communication needs, 20–22, 32–33
  initial interaction mechanisms, 25–26
Attention getters,
  communicative need, 22
  evaluation, 36, 38
  misuse, 39
  necessity, 38
  types, 36, *37*
Augmentative communication system,
  aids, 4
  components evaluation, 27
    accessibilty, 31
    assertability, 29, 32, 41, 57
    display permanence, 30, 32, 42, 47
    flexibility, 31, 32
    independence, 29, 32, 42, 57
    message correctability, 30, 42
    message intelligibility, 27–28, 32, 42, 46
    message production rate, 28, 32, 41, 46, 57
    openness/expandability, 31
    projection ability, 29, 32, 42, 46, 57
    sample assessment, 32–33
  professionals' role, 9–11

strategies, 4
transmission techniques, 3

B

Blissymbols, use with communication aids, *66, 67*, 101, *101*

C

Codes. *See* Encoding.
Communication aids,
  electronic categories, 6
  features, 4–5
  mounting, 117, 124, *130*
    accessibility, 124–125
    custom made equipment, 127, 131, *131*
    design and evaluation guidelines, 127–129
    sources, 126, *126*, 127
    trial period importance, 125
  nonelectronic necessity, 15–16
  portability, 117
    categories, 118, *119*
    communication need factor, 120
    mismatching, 122
    user mobility factor, 120–121, 123
    user preference, 121
  symbols use, 98
    Blissymbols, 101, *101*
    Picsyms, 102, *102*
    pictographs, 100, *100*

Italic page numbers refer to figures and tables.

Encoding,
    abbreviations, 85
    code chart placement, 86, *86*
    control switches use, 94
    direct selection, 81-83, *84*
    and electronic aids, 84
    eye gaze systems, 81-83, *82*
    levels use, 87, *87*
    MINSPEAK system, 88-89, *89*
    Morse code use, 85
    and nonelectronic aids, 84
Eye gaze,
    with direct selection
        techniques, 64-65, *64*
    with encoding techniques,
        81-83, *82*

G

Group-item scanning, 70, *71*

H

Head movement,
    and control switches, 93, *93*
    with direct selection
        techniques, 62-64, *63*

I

Iconic communication system.
    See MINSPEAK.
Interaction, mechanisms
    establishment, 26-27

K

Keyboard emulating interface,
    138

L

Linear scanning, 70-71, *71*
    control switch use, 93-94, *94*

M

Microcomputers. *See* Computers.
MINSPEAK, 88-89, *89*
Morse code, and encoding
    techniques, 85
Mounting, of communication
    aids, 117, 124, *130*
    accessibility, 124-125
    custom-made equipment, 127,
        131, *131*
    design and evaluation
        guidelines, 127-129
    sources, 126, *126*
    trial period importance, 125

N

Nonelectronic communication
    aids,
    direct selection techniques,
        62-70
        electronic comparison, 69-70
        eye gaze, 64-65, *64*
        head movement, 62-64, *63*
        individual development,
            65-66, *66*, *67*
    necessity, 15-16, 18
    scanning, 70-71, *70*
    visual selection, 40-42, *41*

P

Picsyms, in communication aids,
    102, *102*
Pictographs, in communication
    aids, 100, *100*, 113
Portability, of communication
    aids,
    categories, 118, *119*
    communication need factor,
        120
    mismatching, 122
    user mobility factor, 120-121,
        123
    user preference, 121
Positioning of disabled person, in
    selection technique choice,
    77, 80

Printers,
    evaluation, 56–57
    types, 52, 55, *55*
    use examples, 57–59

S

Scanning techniques,
    advantages, 74
    control switch use, 93–94, *94*
    disadvantages, *74*
    electronic, 72–73, *72*
    group-item, 70, *71*
    linear, 70–71, *71*
    nonelectronic, 70–71, *71*, 73
Selection techniques, choice
        considerations,
    positioning, 77–78
    target areas arrangement, 78
Speech output aids,
    evaluation, 46–47
    programmable aids, 47
    selection considerations, 48–49
        intelligibility, 49
        partner comprehension,
            48–49
        user manipulation, 48
    spelling instruction use, 50
    synthesized speech use, 45
    visual impairment applications,
        51
Speech/writing-impaired
        individual,
    characteristics, 7–8
    communication needs
            determination, 20–22
    communication partner, 8–9
        limitations, 27
    expectations of electronic aids,
        13–14
    overall augmentative
            communication system, 2
    resistance to electronic aids,
        12–13
    writing needs determination,
        23–24
Switches, in electronic
        communication aids, 91
    compatibility, 95
    multiple function capability, 95
    purchase factors, 96
    selection, 94

single and multiple switch use,
        93–94, *94*
    varieties, 91–93, *91*, *92*, *93*
Symbols, use with communication
        aids,
    Blissymbols, *66*, *67*, 101, *101*
    Picsyms, 102, *102*
    pictographs, 100, *100*, 113
    selection considerations, 98–99
    text-to-speech programs,
        105–106, *106*

T

Therapists, role in augmented
        communication program,
        9–11

U

Unaided scanning technique, 3

V

Visual displays,
    evaluation, 56–57
    types, 52–55, *53*, *54*, *55*
    use examples, 57–59
Visual selection,
    electronic, 43–44, *43*
        effectiveness, *43*
    nonelectronic, 40–42, *41*
        assertability, 41
        communication rate, 41
        correctability, 42
        dependence drawback, 42
        display permanence, 42
        emotional emphasis, 41
Vocabularies, of communication
        aids,
    item selection, 111–113,
        115–116
    multiple functions, 113, *114*
    open versus fixed, 108–110,
        109, *110*
    programming, 109–111

W

Writing,
    needs determination, *23–24*
    skill importance, *7–8*